P9-CFE-879

For current pricing information,
or to learn more about this or any Nextext title,
call us toll-free at **1-800-323-5435**
or visit our web site at www.nextext.com.

STORIES IN HISTORY

THE MIDDLE AGES

350–1450

Printed in the United States of America

ISBN 0-618-14221-5

2 3 4 5 6 7 — QKT — 06 05 04 03 02 01

Table of Contents

The Roman Empire is ruled by four men, two in the east and two in the west. The two in the west are at war. The western ruler Constantine has a vision that not only affects his army but changes world history.

Attila and his warring horsemen attack the borders of the Western Roman Empire. Do they dare to attack Rome itself?

PART III: SAINTS AND SINNERS

About This Book

The stories are historical fiction. They are based on historical fact, but some of the characters and events may be fictional. In the Sources section you'll learn which is which and where the information came from.

The illustrations are all historical. If they are from a time different from the story, the caption tells you. Original documents help you understand the time period. Maps let you know where things were.

Items explained in People and Terms to Know are repeated in the Glossary. Look there if you come across a name or term you don't know.

Historians do not always agree on the exact dates of events in the ancient past. The letter c *before a date, means "about" (from the Latin word* circa).

If you would like to read more about these exciting times, you will find recommendations in Reading on Your Own.

Background

> It happened on a day in the spring
> When I had stopped at the Tabard Inn
> Ready to set out on my pilgrimage
> To Canterbury with a very faithful heart,
> At night were come into the inn
> A company of nine and twenty people
> Of various types, by chance arrived
> Together, and pilgrims they were all . . .

Geoffrey Chaucer,
"Prologue," from *The Canterbury Tales*

▲
Chaucer's Canterbury pilgrims gather around the table in an inn.

The Decline of Rome

In A.D. 330, the Roman Emperor Constantine moved his capital from Rome to the city of Byzantium on the Black Sea. This city was given a new name, Constantinople, "city of Constantine." After Constantine's death, the empire was divided into an eastern part centered at Constantinople and a western part centered at Rome. The Western Empire fell in 476. Its fall began a period of European history called the Middle Ages, or medieval (MEE•dee•EE•vuhl) period. This period lasted until about 1500. During these centuries, Europeans produced wonderful works of literature, philosophy, and art. However, the Middle Ages were also troubled by ignorance, superstition, war, and disease.

Barbarian Invasions

One cause for the decline of the Western Empire was attacks by Germanic people from eastern Europe. The Visigoths, Vandals, and Franks were among them. Another group, the Huns from central Asia, also attacked the Western Empire. In 410 the Visigoths attacked Rome itself. In 452, Rome was threatened again, this time by the Huns under Attila. Rome was spared when the pope convinced Attila to withdraw. In 455, Rome was attacked again, this time by the Vandals. In 476, the last Roman emperor, a 14-year-old boy named Romulus Augustulus, was removed from the throne by a Germanic general. Roman power in the West had ended.

The Byzantine Empire

The Eastern Empire would last for over 1,000 years. It was called *Byzantine* (BIHZ•uhn•TEEN), after the original name of its capital, Byzantium. The Byzantine rulers saw themselves as Roman emperors. Like the Caesars, the Byzantine emperors ruled with absolute power. They also lived with the constant threat of violence. Of the 88 Byzantine emperors, 29 died violently. One of the greatest Byzantine emperors, Justinian, was nearly driven

▲
The Byzantine empress Theodora stands with some of the people of her court.

from his throne. It was in 532, when mobs burned much of Constantinople during the Nika Revolt. Justinian was talked out of fleeing the capital by his brave wife, Theodora. One of Justinian's greatest acts was the Code of Justinian. This single body of law was based on Roman laws. Justinian's Code served the Byzantine Empire for hundreds of years. When Constantinople fell to the Ottoman Turks in 1453, the Eastern Roman Empire came to an end.

Charlemagne

During the late 400s, a Germanic people known as the Franks had built a large kingdom in the former Roman province of Gaul. By three centuries later, under the Frankish ruler Charlemagne (SHAHR•luh•MAYN) or "Charles the Great," this kingdom had grown much greater. Charlemagne ruled much of western Europe. His empire began to rival that of the old Western Roman Empire. In 800, Pope Leo III crowned Charlemagne emperor. However, Charlemagne's empire broke up quickly under the weak rulers who followed him. One of the lasting things that Charlemagne did was to encourage learning. He surrounded himself with English, German, Italian, and Spanish scholars. He opened a palace school at his capital of Aachen (AH•kuhn).

Medieval Europe, 800–1000

Vikings

Between 800 and 1000, a new threat came from northern Europe. These invaders were a Germanic people known as Vikings or Northmen. They were skillful sailors and fierce warriors. The Vikings used their swift warships to carry out terrifying raids on the people of western Europe. These attacks helped to weaken Charlemagne's empire. The Christians of the Viking era prayed, "From the wrath of the Northmen, O Lord deliver us."

Islam and Christianity

The Rise of Islam

In 613, an Arabian prophet named Muhammad (muh•HAM•ihd) began to preach a new faith, Islam. His followers were known as Muslims. By the time Muhammad died in 632, his followers controlled much of Arabia. (See map on page 76.) In the hundred years after his death, Muslim armies

◀ Islam's heaven is a beautiful garden on seven levels.

conquered a huge empire. It stretched from the Atlantic Ocean to India. Within the boundaries of the Islamic empire, there was a rich civilization. The cultures of many different peoples contributed to this civilization. Trade expanded. Great works of literature and art were created. There were advances in mathematics, medicine, and other sciences. Muslims also made a major contribution to medieval European civilization by preserving ancient Greek learning.

The Crusades

Throughout the Middle Ages, Muslims and Christians often fought each other. In 1096, Pope Urban II issued a call for what he termed a "holy war." The pope asked the Christian princes of Europe to take back control of Jerusalem and the Holy Land from the Muslim Turks. Over the next 200 years, Europeans went on a long series of such holy wars, called the Crusades. The First Crusade succeeded in capturing Jerusalem in 1099. By 1187, however, the city was once again in Muslim hands. In the 1200s, Crusades were frequent but unsuccessful. The religious spirit of the First Crusade had faded, replaced by a search for personal gain.

What Life Was Like

Almost everyone in the Middle Ages belonged to one of four groups: the nobility, the Church, the merchants and craftsmen, and the peasants.

The Nobility

At the top of the medieval social order was the king. He gave land to his nobles, who gave him an army of knights in return. Throughout most of the Middle Ages, heavily armed knights on huge warhorses were what won wars. When knights were not involved in actual combat, they practiced in war games called tournaments.

▲
Knights practiced for combat by fighting in tournaments.

▲
Before the invention of printing, monks copied books by hand.

The Church

In the Middle Ages, the Church controlled other areas of life besides religion. One of the most important of these was learning. After the fall of the Western Empire, much ancient learning had been lost. Some learning was saved in monasteries. In the monasteries, monks opened schools, kept libraries, and copied books. Monks made careful copies of ancient writings. They decorated their books with beautiful lettering and pictures. In the 1100s, people became more interested in learning. They started a new kind of school—the university. Most students at universities were sons of merchants or skilled workers.

Merchants and Craftsmen

During the Middle Ages, trade increased and towns grew. More people became merchants. Trade routes spread across Europe, and Italian merchant ships traveled the Mediterranean to ports in the Byzantine Empire such as Constantinople. Skilled workers made goods by hand for local or long-distance trade. These workers were members of guilds. A guild was a group of people who worked at the same trade or craft. Guilds controlled all wages and prices in their craft. The families of the merchants and skilled workers formed the beginnings of a middle class.

A merchant examines the precious stones she sells. ▶

▲

Peasants work in the fields below the castle of their lord.

Peasants

In the Middle Ages, most people were peasants. Most peasants were serfs. Serfs were people who could not legally leave the estate of the lord they worked for. The estate, called a manor, usually covered only a few square miles of land. Generally, 15 to 30 families lived in the village on the manor. The peasants raised or produced nearly everything that they and their lord needed for daily life—food, fuel, cloth, leather goods, and lumber.

The End of the Middle Ages

This scourge had implanted so great a terror in the hearts of men and women that brothers abandoned brothers, uncles their nephews, sisters their brothers, and in many cases wives deserted their husbands. But even worse, . . . fathers and mothers refused to nurse and assist their own children.

—Giovanni Boccaccio,
on the Black Death

▲

Plague victims appear in a painting titled *The Triumph of Death*.

Beginning in the 1300s, medieval society was seriously weakened by a series of events. These included the Great Schism, the Black Death, and the Hundred Years' War.

The Great Schism (SIHZ•uhm) was a split in the government of the Church. For a time there were two popes, and later, even three.

A deadly disease known as the bubonic plague, or Black Death, struck Western Europe in 1347. This plague killed one-third of the population. As town populations fell, trade declined and prices rose. Serfs left their manors.

Between 1337 and 1453, England and France fought the Hundred Years' War to decide who would occupy the French throne. This brutal struggle was fought out on French soil. By 1420, France appeared defeated. Then, in 1429, a French peasant girl named Joan of Arc claimed to hear heavenly voices directing her to rescue her country from English invaders. Joan inspired the French to resist. Soon, however, she was captured by her enemies and burned at the stake. France finally won the war, but was left exhausted. Under the impact of this series of disasters, the medieval way of life began to disappear.

Time Line

330—Roman emperor Constantine moves his capital to Byzantium, which he renames Constantinople.

452—Attila invades Italy but does not attack Rome.

476—Western Roman Empire falls.

c. 529—Benedict founds the abbey of Monte Cassino.

532—Nika Revolt in Constantinople nearly drives the emperor Justinian from his throne.

622—Muhammad flees from Mecca to Medina. This flight marks the start of the Islamic calendar.

800—Charlemagne is crowned emperor by the pope.

991—Vikings defeat English at the battle of Maldon.

1099—European warriors of the First Crusade capture Jerusalem from its Muslim defenders.

1215—King John of England signs the Magna Carta.

1273—Thomas Aquinas completes his *Summa Theologica*.

1337–1453—The Hundred Years' War is fought between England and France.

1347–1351—The Black Death kills a third of the people of Europe.

c. 1387—Chaucer begins *The Canterbury Tales.*

1429—Joan of Arc leads the French at Orléans.

1453—Constantinople falls to the Ottoman Turks.

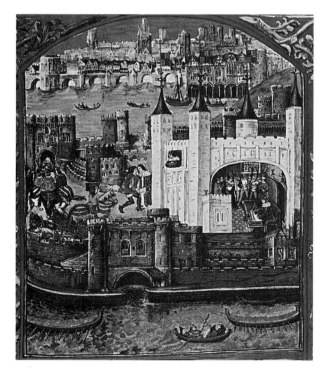

▲

London is shown as it appeared during the Hundred Years' War in this illustration from a medieval manuscript.

The Decline
of Rome

An Emperor's Vision

BY DEE MASTERS

The vast army sweeps its way through the mountain passes that separate Italy from the rest of Europe. Eight **legions** are on the march. Eight silver war eagles sitting atop their long poles lead the way. Forty thousand men follow. Their strong hobnailed sandals move quickly. These men are veterans of Rome's constant frontier wars. Metal helmets and chest armor reflect the cold mountain sun. Each man carries a dagger, a short sword, two long spears for stabbing and throwing, and a tall shield. These are professional soldiers who have signed up for twenty-five years of service. They go where

People and Terms to Know

legions (LEE•juhns)—companies of 3,000 to 6,000 foot soldiers and 300 to 700 men on horseback.

A Roman cavalry charge is shown on this panel from the Arch of Constantine.

they are told. And their leader, their Caesar, **Constantine**, has told them they will cross these mountains and will march into Rome itself.

The Roman Empire is governed by four men, two in the east and two in the west. Everyone knows that **Maxentius**, who controls Rome, has been preparing to invade the far western part of the Roman Empire. That part is controlled by Constantine. Maxentius has proven himself cruel and greedy. He has declared that he alone is emperor.

This march is different. Legions are not supposed to enter Rome.

The Roman officer Caius has kept the eighty men under his command in good spirits. They have moved fast, though they have eaten their bread, cheese, and beans washed down with wine and jokes. Caius trusts his men and his emperor. It is good to be under a leader who has so often and so recently led his men into battle successfully. This march is different. Legions are not supposed to enter Rome. Caius will be fighting

People and Terms to Know

Constantine (KAHN•stuhn•TEEN)—(c. 285–337) Roman emperor from 306 to 337. He moved the capital east to Constantinople, ended persecution of Christians, and supported the spread of Christianity.

Maxentius (mak•SEHN•shee•uhs)—co-ruler with Constantine of the Western Roman Empire. He controlled Italy and Rome itself.

Romans unlike himself. Those Romans will be soft, too used to eating good food, going to the **circus**, not fighting.

Caius has heard that secret messengers have come from Rome and from the senate asking for Constantine's help. Caius's lieutenant Titus says that there are no secrets in the legions.

The head of this great snake of an army has wound its way out of the mountains and descended into the plains of northwest Italy. Although there may be no secrets in the legions, in Rome Maxentius doesn't know that Constantine's forces are about to challenge him.

At the foot of the mountains stands a powerful walled city that guards the stone roads leading to Rome. The day they arrive, Constantine's legions set fire to the city's gates and scale the walls. The city falls. There is no pause for victory. Forty miles away the legions meet heavy **cavalry**. But the experienced Constantine has a defense that confuses and divides them. He wins again.

People and Terms to Know

circus—place where large entertainments were put on free for the Roman public.

cavalry (KAV•uhl•ree)—soldiers who fight on horseback.

Caius and Titus complain that night. There is no wine to wash down their bread and beans and very little cheese. But there are two excellent Roman roads they can use to cover the 400 miles to Rome. Although they are tired, Constantine's soldiers will need to move fast, because they are running out of food. If Maxentius hides behind the walls of Rome, Caius and the rest of Constantine's legions will have to withdraw. They won't have anything to eat.

In Rome, people are rioting because Maxentius refuses to lead the troops in battle. They think he is pretending that Constantine is not a threat. They believe Maxentius doesn't want to cause alarm.

◀ This head of Constantine was once part of a seated image of the emperor that was over thirty feet high.

Maxentius is forced to meet Constantine. He gathers his legions nine miles outside of Rome with the river Tiber behind him. Maxentius is confident. He has four times as many soldiers as Constantine and is well supplied. His men are fresh.

Caius and Titus hear the rumors being whispered in the tense camp. Constantine sent for the priests who examine the livers of sacrificed animals to discover what will happen. The priests say that Constantine will be defeated. Many of the men in camp are afraid. Caius is a Christian. He believes the Roman gods are false. He also knows that many of the men will, however, believe the predictions.

Caius is a Christian. He believes the Roman gods are false.

Another nearby officer has caught one of his men deserting. A man like this might cause danger to men in battle. The other soldiers stone the coward to death. The spirit of Constantine's legions is very low. They are heavily outnumbered, and the gods are against them. Soon, many may desert.

Titus brings a new rumor that is sweeping through the camp. Constantine has experienced a miracle, a personal sign from the Christian god! Titus reports that people are saying Constantine saw a brilliant light near the sun with the cross and the first two letters of Christ's name in it. Some say that the Christian god promised Constantine he would conquer under this sign.

Almost immediately messengers arrive. Caius and his men must carve the cross and the initials of Christ on their shields. There is a great change of mood in the camp. There is a god on their side! He has spoken personally to their leader. Caius feels he is fighting now for something greater than political gain. Perhaps if Constantine fights under the sign of Christ, he will end the frequent **persecution** of Christians after the war is over!

The next day the two armies meet. Maxentius's army deserts their unpopular emperor. His soldiers run wildly back toward Rome. The special bridge Maxentius built to bring his troops across the Tiber collapses. Many drown in the deep and fast flowing river. Maxentius himself is pulled under the water by the weight of his heavy armor and drowns. Constantine is the emperor of the Western Empire and of Rome!

People and Terms to Know

persecution (PUHR•sih•KYOO•shuhn)—bad treatment of people because of their principles or beliefs.

Caius is filled with joy. They have won a great victory and now have a Christian emperor. Titus also celebrates. Titus isn't sure whether there had been a vision, but he is sure that the emperor Constantine knows how to inspire men.

QUESTIONS TO CONSIDER

1. Why do you think men fought for control of the Roman Empire?

2. Why does Caius think it will be easy to defeat the soldiers in Rome?

3. How can you tell that Constantine was an experienced general?

4. What are some reasons why soldiers would desert the army of Constantine?

5. What does this story tell you about the condition of the Roman Empire at the time Constantine defeated Maxentius?

Attila and the Pope

BY WALTER HAZEN

Many years have passed since that day in 452 on the Mincio River near the northern Italian city of Mantua. If I live to be a hundred, however, I will never forget the importance of what took place there. The very survival of Western civilization was at stake, and we knew it at the time.

I will also never forget my first look at the man we had gone there to meet. He was the most frightful person I have ever seen. He had a large head, a flat nose, and shoulders that were too broad for his short body. He seemed to delight in rolling his eyes and causing anyone who saw him to be afraid. I shuddered as I awaited whatever was about to happen.

This is how an artist in the 1800s pictured Attila's invasion of Italy.

I speak of **Attila**, king of the **Huns**. Throughout Europe, he had the name "Scourge of God." I must say that the name was well-deserved. He was without doubt the fiercest fighter of our times. He destroyed cities and killed their people. He and his men fought with bows and arrows while riding at full speed on their strong horses. Anyone unlucky enough to be caught was dragged off with a rope around his neck. Even some of the **barbaric** Germans feared him. Many of them looked for safety inside our very borders. Until his huge army was turned back in 451 at the Battle of Chalons in **Gaul**, he had overrun much of eastern and central Europe.

To keep themselves fed, the Huns stole food and killed animals wherever they found them. Above all, however, they wanted gold. Give them gold, and they might return their prisoners or they might not destroy your town.

People and Terms to Know

Attila (AT•uhl•uh)—(c.406–453) king of the Huns after 434. He destroyed cities from the Danube River in central and eastern Europe to the Rhine River in Germany. A scourge is someone or something that causes great trouble.

Huns—nomadic warring people from north-central Asia who occupied China. About 370, they moved west.

barbaric (bahr•BAR•ihk)—not civilized; rude and wild. According to the Romans, anyone who lived outside the Roman Empire was barbaric or a barbarian.

Gaul (gawl)—ancient region of western Europe that was part of the Roman Empire. It included all of what is now France and surrounding areas.

One year after leaving Gaul, Attila turned his attention to Italy. He crossed the Alps and easily took many cities in northern Italy. The road to Rome lay open before him. He boasted that he would take it and present it as a gift to his bride-to-be Honoria. Honoria was the sister of our emperor of Rome, Valentinian III.

We Romans were in no position to stop Attila's advance.

A few years before the Hun invasion, he tried to force her to marry a man she hated. To avoid this, she sent her ring to Attila and asked for his help. Attila thought this was a proposal of marriage, and he set out for Italy to claim his bride.

We Romans were in no position to stop Attila's advance. After the Battle of Chalons the year before, our leaders had a hard time raising an army. Emperor Valentinian, knowing that his troops stood little chance against the Huns, asked for help from the **Vatican**. He asked His Holiness, Pope **Leo I**, to go to Attila's camp and beg him to spare our city.

People and Terms to Know

Vatican (VAT•ih•kuhn)—government of the pope in Rome; also the buildings that house the pope.

Leo I—(c. 400–461) pope known as "Leo the Great." He was pope from 440 to 461. He saved Rome from an invasion of the Huns in 452. He persuaded the leader of the Vandals, a German tribe, to spare the city again three years later.

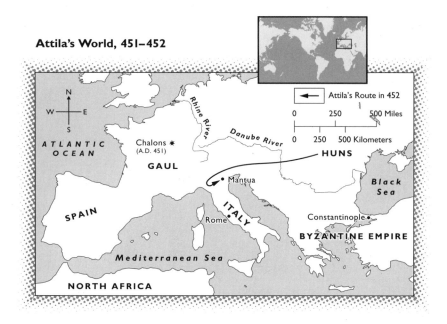

Here is where I come into the story. I, along with the **consul** Avienus and others, went with His Holiness to Mantua (MAN•choo•uh). What an amusing sight we must have presented to the Huns. Dressed in brightly colored robes, we wore no armor and carried no weapons. A few swift sword thrusts would have seen us dead in seconds. Surely Attila thought we were fools.

His Holiness, however, never lost faith that heaven would protect us. He fearlessly approached

People and Terms to Know

consul—official of the Roman government.

Attila and began to speak. He told the barbarian leader that our city was at his mercy and helpless before his army. He flattered him by calling him the "king of kings" who had conquered many people. He then challenged him to "conquer himself" and show mercy toward us.

To everyone's surprise, Attila did not attack Rome. He turned his great army around and left Italy. He went north, where he again attacked Gaul. Why did he leave? Why did he bow to the pope's plea? No one knows for certain, but there are several opinions.

One opinion is that Attila was impressed by the dress and splendor of his Christian visitors. I personally have little faith in this explanation. Attila may have been impressed by our colorful clothes, but this was probably not enough to keep him from killing us like so many sheep.

Another belief held by many is that as the pope began to talk to Attila, images of Saint Peter and Saint Paul appeared at his side. Both were armed with swords. They threatened to kill the Hun if he did not spare Rome. Perhaps this really happened. Who am I to say it did not?

A final idea is that Attila simply ran out of supplies. This is the explanation our historians seem to prefer. There had been a food shortage a year earlier. Attila's army could find little to eat in our countryside. In addition, a **plague** had swept through his forces and greatly reduced their numbers. Certainly these two causes were enough to make the mighty conqueror withdraw.

Whatever the cause, Attila went away and left Rome untouched. Valentinian refused to let Honoria go to Attila. I heard later that the Hun married someone else. Since he already had several wives, I suppose he didn't mind losing the emperor's sister.

There was talk that Attila planned another invasion for the following year, but he died before he could carry it out. As for our small group, we returned to Rome, where His Holiness was hailed as a hero.

QUESTIONS TO CONSIDER

1. What made the Huns so feared?
2. Why do you think the Huns had to steal and kill for food?
3. How did Pope Leo persuade Attila to change his mind?
4. Why do you think Attila did not attack Rome?

People and Terms to Know

plague (playg)—disease that spreads quickly and usually causes death. One of the worst kinds of plague is the bubonic plague, which is caused by fleas carried by rats.

A Bear-Keeper's Daughter

BY STEPHEN FEINSTEIN

It was the year 533, in the days of the Eastern Roman Empire. Juliana, the spinner of wool, made her way through the noisy midday crowds in the marketplace of the city of Constantinople. Far in the distance she could see the roofs of the great palace of Emperor **Justinian** and Empress **Theodora**.

Juliana kept glancing back to make sure nobody was following her. She was still not used to the idea that she was no longer a slave. Indeed, she was now a free woman, thanks to one person—the Empress Theodora.

People and Terms to Know

Justinian (juh•STIHN•ee•un)—(483–565) brilliant emperor of the Eastern Empire from 527 to 565. He was a great builder, and the preserver of Roman law for future generations.

Theodora (thee•uh•DAW•ruh)—(c. 508–548) wife of the emperor Justinian. She had great influence over him and over the political and religious events of their rule.

This portrait of Empress Theodora is a detail from the picture on page 11.

When Juliana reached the edge of the marketplace, she came upon a row of two-story buildings. She stopped at a small shop and timidly knocked on the door. An old man with a long white beard opened the door. "Yes, what can I do for you?" he asked.

Juliana looked inside the shop and saw shelves filled with scrolls of **parchment**. "Are you Thanasis the **scribe**?" asked Juliana. When the old man nodded, she continued, "I have need of your services. I need to send a letter."

Thanasis looked carefully at her, squinting in puzzlement. The woman before him looked to be poor. "Don't you know that my services cost money?" he said. "How can a person such as yourself possibly afford to pay me? You'd be better off writing the letter yourself."

"Do you think I would be standing here now if I knew how to write?" asked Juliana. She reached into her robe and held out two gold coins. "I have been saving these coins for a very long time—for just such an occasion."

People and Terms to Know

parchment—skin of a sheep or goat prepared as a material on which to write.

scribe—in ancient times, a public clerk. People who did not know how to read or write would use a scribe to help them.

Thanasis nodded again and said, "I guess you have a very important message to send. To whom should I address this letter?"

"To the Empress Theodora!" said Juliana.

Thanasis stared at her in shock. "Are you mad, woman?" he cried. "How dare you even think of such a thing! The royal family does not welcome **petitions** from poor folk. Why, you could be arrested, or even worse! I could even be putting myself in danger."

Juliana was becoming annoyed. "I do not wish to send a petition or make a request!" she said angrily. "I simply wish to send a thank-you letter. I tried to enter the palace to speak to the empress in person, but the guards at the gate chased me away. Perhaps this will help put your mind at ease," she said, holding out a third gold coin. "Take this coin also. It is my last one."

Thanasis's manner abruptly changed. The old Greek invited Juliana to sit down with him at his writing desk. In a kindly voice, he said, "I will help

---

People and Terms to Know

petitions (puh•TISH•uns)—formal requests for rights or benefits from an authority.

you. But first, I would like to know why on earth you feel the need to write to such a powerful woman. Don't you remember what happened in our city last year? Don't you know that it was Theodora's orders that resulted in the deaths of 30,000 of our citizens?"

"Of course I've not forgotten the killings," Juliana answered. "Perhaps *you* have forgotten the riots and fires that prompted the killings. The rebels were the ones who rioted and started the fires. They were planning to overthrow the emperor! People say the emperor's advisors urged him to flee for his life. Only Theodora advised him to stay and save his empire. Then he ordered General **Belisarius** to put an end to the revolt. The rebels had gathered in the **Hippodrome**, you know. That's where they were killed. But I have other memories of the Hippodrome, much happier memories."

They were planning to overthrow the emperor!

People and Terms to Know

Belisarius (BEHL•ih•SAIR•ee•uhs)—(505–565) powerful general, whose loyalty to Justinian and Theodora prevented rebels from overthrowing them in 532.

Hippodrome—stadium in Constantinople seating 60,000 spectators and offering free entertainment, such as chariot races and trained animal acts.

"What do you mean?" asked Thanasis.

"When I was a little girl, I had a friend whose father, Akakios, was a bear-keeper. My friend and I used to play together while Akakios trained the animals for the shows in the Hippodrome. We were poor, but we were happy. When Akakios died, my friend became a dancer and an actress. She was very smart and had a wonderful talent for acting. The crowds loved her. I used to see her perform before the people in the Hippodrome. My friend even tried to teach me how to act, and for a while we worked together. But I was not as gifted as she was, and our paths drifted apart. She became popular with the richest citizens of Constantinople. She traveled to distant lands, where her fame went before her. Eventually, she met Justinian, nephew of the old Emperor Justin, and—"

"Let me guess," Thanasis interrupted. As Juliana was speaking, Thanasis's eyes had grown wide. "Your friend—was Theodora!" he blurted.

"Yes, Theodora," said Juliana. "And Justinian and Theodora fell in love! It still seems so amazing to me that my old friend, whose father was a bear-keeper, could become the most powerful woman in the empire."

"Especially when you consider that there was a law against a poor person marrying a rich one," added Thanasis.

"But Justinian requested that the law be changed, and the emperor granted the request," said Juliana. "The two were married. And when the old emperor died, Justinian and Theodora became emperor and empress."

"But I still fail to see why you must write to the empress now," said Thanasis.

Juliana looked at Thanasis and smiled. "I would not be sitting here today, if not for the empress. Years ago, I had been sold into slavery, like many other unfortunate young women from poor families. Last week, I was about to be shipped off to a life of dreadful hardship in a faraway desert kingdom. The very day before the ship was to sail, my master told me I was now a free woman. I learned that Theodora had bought my freedom, as she had done for so many other women. I also learned that she had persuaded Justinian to pass laws to protect women's rights. Now, daughters as well as sons can inherit property. So you see, I want Theodora to know how grateful I am."

"Why don't we begin writing now," said the old scribe. "Tell me what you wish to say to the empress." He rolled out a blank sheet of parchment and prepared his writing tools.

Juliana began to dictate her letter. "My dear Empress Theodora," she began. "My old friend, thank you for giving me—my life!"

QUESTIONS TO CONSIDER

1. Why did the scribe agree to write a letter for Juliana?
2. Why did Juliana want to write to Theodora?
3. What different sides of Theodora's life are revealed in Juliana's story?
4. How would you describe the empress Theodora?

The Trolley to Yesterday
by John Bellairs

John Bellairs's time-travel story tells of a trip to Constantinople in the Middle Ages. Young Johnny Dixon and his friend Professor Childermass discover a trolley that carries them back to Constantinople in 1453 as the Turks are invading the Byzantine Empire.

The Byzantine Empire
by James A. Corrick

James A. Corrick presents the history of the Byzantine Empire and its influence on the civilization of Europe.

Anna of Byzantium
by Tracy Barrett

Tracy Barrett's historical novel is based on the life of Anna Comnena, the daughter of eleventh-century Byzantine emperor Alexius I. Anna tells her own story of struggle for power in the emperor's palace at Constantinople.

Work—*The Rule* of St. Benedict

BY DEE MASTERS

Yes, people said there were **miracles**. But the old **monk** felt that the miracles got in his way. People thought about the miracles instead of the work. The work was what mattered. Now the work was done. Six days before, the old monk had told his brothers that he was dying. He told them to open his grave. The fever almost burned him up. He took the **bread and wine**. He wanted to die as he had lived, and he was ready to die.

People and Terms to Know

miracles—unusual events that cannot be explained by science.
monk—man who gives up worldly things and enters a monastery to live a religious life.
bread and wine—very small amount of food and drink used in the Christian Communion, a ceremony to remember Christ's last supper.

<u>Benedict</u> and his twin sister had been born in 480 as the Western Roman Empire fell apart. At age twenty, he went to Rome to finish his studies. There, he found the other students only wanted money and fun. He wanted to serve God. He wanted to be with other people who wanted to serve God. His studies were not enough. He could not find what he wanted in Rome. He left the city and in the hills forty miles away from Rome, he found a small group of men and women who were seeking as he was seeking.

One day his old nurse who had gone with him broke a kitchen strainer. She was very upset and cried. Benedict prayed over the strainer. It became like new, unbroken! Word of this miracle spread. The strainer was fastened to the church door. People came from all around to see it and the man who had made it whole. They wanted more miracles. Benedict could not do his work. He could not reach out to God. Benedict felt he had failed.

He left again and went into the mountains, past a great lake, into a narrow valley. He went up and

---

People and Terms to Know

Benedict (BEHN•ih•DIHKT)—(c. 480–c. 547) Italian monk and founder of the Benedictine order of monks. His *Rule* became a guidebook for monks for centuries.

up. At the end of his path was a cliff with a cave about ten feet deep. For three years Benedict lived in the cave, alone. He thought and prayed.

People heard about how seriously Benedict was trying to reach God. They came to get Benedict's help. A group of monks asked him to lead them. But what he asked was too hard for them, so Benedict returned to his cave. He had

People heard about how seriously Benedict was trying to reach God.

failed, but he had learned about himself and others. He couldn't ask people to do too much too soon. It scared them away. He still was reaching out for his God, but now he knew he wanted to help others who were also reaching out.

Next, Benedict tried starting twelve small communities, each with twelve monks and an older monk to help them. Each community was modeled on Christ and his twelve followers. Benedict's monks did so well that some other religious communities became jealous. Benedict again felt he had failed to serve God.

But he had learned. This time he was ready. His failures helped him to see clearly how he could succeed. He had read, studied, thought, lived, and failed. This time he would build a great **monastery**. He built it on the top of a mountain, **Monte Cassino**. He built it away from people who might be jealous. But he built it where people could easily reach it.

While he built, he wrote *The Rule*. He gave "advice from a father who loves you." In this little guidebook, he called for people to wake up from their sleep. He asked whether there was anyone "who yearns for life and desires to see good days." He shared what he had learned. *The Rule* became the guidebook for monks throughout Europe during the Middle Ages.

Benedict meant Monte Cassino and **The Rule** *to help people reach for God.*

Benedict meant Monte Cassino and *The Rule* to help people reach for God. Benedict asked people to work. He wanted people to live together and help each other as if they were a family. No one at Monte Cassino could own anything, and they had to work

People and Terms to Know

monastery (MAHN•uh•STEHR•ee)—community or building where monks live.

Monte Cassino (MAHN•tee kuh•SEE•noh)—mountain in Italy. The town of Cassino and the famous monastery were reduced to rubble during World War II.

and help others. Benedict asked his fellow seekers to spend time together in prayer. He asked them to memorize prayers and study sacred writings. Everyone read and studied at least four hours a day. They worked to grow their own food. They taught children and visitors. Benedict asked them to act as if Jesus was with them at all times, as if every person with them was Jesus. At Monte Cassino people worked together to help each other live good lives.

Benedict followed his *Rule*. He carried water, worked in the fields, read and studied, prayed, taught, welcomed strangers, and gave what he had to the poor and sick. He gently helped monks who could not concentrate on their work and prayers.

Nevertheless, people talked about his miracles. They said that he had removed a heavy stone that the monks couldn't move. They said he had brought a boy back to life who had been crushed under a heavy wall. They claimed he could see what people were doing far away from him, make food appear in a famine, and cure leprosy. These miracles and more, people reported, but Benedict never wrote about them. Miracles were not important to him. Work was.

◀ This example of an illuminated manuscript shows a decorated capital letter *D*.

His community of seekers became the Benedictine monks. When Rome burned, when the great libraries were destroyed, the Benedictines saved the stories, science, medicine, and thoughts of the past. The books the monks copied by hand were beautifully decorated art works. The brilliant blues, greens, and gold in the paintings and decorations of the books look like a light is shining through them, so they are called "**illuminated manuscripts**." The Benedictine monks and nuns miraculously saved early learning and taught the great books of the past. Benedict would have approved of their work.

People and Terms to Know

illuminated (ih•LOO•muh•NAYT•uhd) **manuscripts**—hand-copied books with very bright lettering and decorations, usually made by monks before the invention of the printing press.

From a wealthy family, as a student in Rome, in a cave in the mountains, as a builder of communities, Benedict had reached out to his God. At the end of his life, while the loving hands of his brother monks held up his weak body, he said a few final words of prayer, his hands reaching up to God, and died in the chapel of the great monastery he had built at Monte Cassino.

QUESTIONS TO CONSIDER

1. Why did Benedict leave Rome?

2. What events made Benedict feel like a failure?

3. Why do you think Benedict's *Rule* is an important book in world history?

The Rule of St. Benedict

22. How the Monks Shall Sleep.

They shall sleep separately in separate
beds. . . . A candle shall always be burning in
that same cell until early in the morning. They
shall sleep clothed, [their robes tied] with belts
or with ropes; and they shall not have their
knives at their sides while they sleep, in case
in a dream they should wound the sleepers. . . .

40. Concerning the Amount of Drink.

Each one has his own gift from God, the one
in this way, the other in that. Therefore it is
with some hesitation that we fix the amount
of daily food and drink. Nevertheless, we
believe that [about a pint] of wine a day is
enough for each one. Those to whom God
gives the ability of [giving up wine] shall
know that they will have their own reward.
But the [monk in charge] shall judge if either
the needs of the place, or labor or the heat of
summer, requires more. . . .

48. Concerning the Daily Manual Labor.

Idleness is the enemy of the soul. And therefore, at fixed times, the brothers ought to be occupied in manual labor; and again, at fixed times, in sacred reading. . . . There shall be appointed one or two elders, who shall go round the monastery at the hours the brothers are reading, and see to it that no troublesome brother may be found who is open to idleness and trifling, and is not intent on his reading; being not only of no use to himself, but also stirring up others.

Viking Raiders

BY JUDITH LLOYD YERO

People call us **Vikings**—a word that strikes fear in their hearts, as well it should. When our great dragon ships appear on the horizon, the result is already known. Quickly, our warriors row their boats to shore and leap out, ready for battle. They are eager for the test of bravery for which they have prepared since childhood. We come for the wealth of the land, for food and drink—for whatever is of value.

They say we are barbarians—bloodthirsty and without mercy. They do not understand that a man's strength is his highest good. Honor, reputation, and the respect of family and friends are

---

People and Terms to Know

Vikings (VY•kihngs)—daring sailors from Scandinavia (Norway, Sweden, and Denmark) who raided the coasts of Europe from around 800 until 1000. They were also called Norsemen or Northmen.

An artist of the 1800s created this picture of a fleet of Viking dragon ships.

what is important in life. Our **sagas** tell what it means to be a Viking.

He held high his shield. He carved his own bows, hunted with hounds. He sat well in the saddle. He used his sword and spear. He swam in the water. He read the **runes** and understood the language of birds, fought for land, and gave away his gold. He guarded the law, married, and had many sons.

Honorable Northmen do not steal. We gain only at the risk of our own lives. We meet our victims face to face. If the enemy's arm is stronger—if his skill with sword and ax and spear is greater—so be it, we die. An honorable death means that we will be forever in **Valhalla**.

Christians call us **heathen**, but our gods give us strength. We believe in the power of the hammer of **Thor**.

People and Terms to Know

sagas (SAH•guhs)—long stories about brave Viking kings and fighters, their families, and their gods.

runes (roons)—letters in an ancient alphabet used by the Scandinavians.

Valhalla (val•HAL•uh)—in Scandinavian mythology, the place where heroes go after death to spend their time eating, drinking, and fighting.

heathen (HEE•thuhn)—people thought to be uncivilized; often used to mean those who are not Christians.

Thor (thawr)—Viking god who rides through the heavens in a chariot drawn by goats, striking rocks with his hammer to create lightning and thunder. Thor's hammer was a symbol of power.

Now, the time has come. The icy cold sea washes across the decks of the dragon ships. The fighting men are weary of the cold and a diet of dried fish and meat. They pull on the oars, eager for battle. I, too, am eager for the story to begin. It is my job to record the tales of our voyage—tales like those of **Ivar the Boneless** and **Erik Bloodaxe** that I will tell around the fire when we return home.

The icy cold sea washes across the decks of the dragon ships.

Among our fighting men are some in search of adventure. Others are landowners with wives and children who tend the crops in their absence. Our great leader is **Olaf Tryggvasson**. His friends are loyal to him, and his enemies fear him greatly. There is no greater honor than to serve with Olaf.

People and Terms to Know

Ivar (EYE•vahr) **the Boneless**—(794–872) Danish Viking leader who ruled Dublin, Ireland, and later captured York in England.

Erik Bloodaxe (died 954)—Viking who was named king of parts of England by the Norwegians.

Olaf Tryggvasson (OH•luhf TRIG•vuh•suhn)—(968–1000) Viking leader who, after many raids on England, was converted to Christianity. After becoming king of Norway in 995, he forced his people to accept Christianity. He drowned while in a battle with Svein Forkbeard, king of Denmark.

◀ This carved wooden head
of a Viking chieftain decorated
a cart found in an ancient
burial site in Norway.

We have already raided English towns to the North. The foolish English king, **Ethelred**, has no stomach for our kind of fighting. His soldiers are better suited to farm the land than to meet us on a field of battle. Though it is against our nature, we have even taken to sparing villages if they agree to pay us **Danegeld**.

People and Terms to Know

Ethelred (EHTH•uhl•REHD)—(c. 968–1016) Ethelred II, called "Ethelred the Unready," king of England from 978 to 1016. His struggles against the Danes were unsuccessful.

Danegeld (DAYN•gehld)—"tax of the Danes," gold, silver, and other goods paid to the Vikings in exchange for not being attacked. The English people were heavily taxed to pay for Danegeld.

Today, we beach our dragon ships in the salt marshes between an island and the English coast. Our men see the pitiful English defenders waiting on the mainland and stand hungry for battle. Our men prefer a fight to the Danegeld, but Olaf calls across to the leader of the English.

"It is better for you that you should attack these spears with gold and silver than that we should fight each other to the death. We need not destroy each other if you are rich enough. We are prepared to make peace in return for the gold."

The English leader replies:

"Sea raider, can you hear what this army is saying? They intend to give you spears and swords. Here stands a fearless leader with his troops. He intends to defend this soil, my King Ethelred's land, its people, and its territory. Let the heathen fall in battle."

No cry is sweeter to the Northmen. They await the outgoing tide that will let them cross the channel to where the defenders wait. At last, the Vikings begin to cross. They are weighed down with weapons. The thick mud of the marshes sucks at their feet, slowing their passage. They are quickly cut down by a few defenders. Clearly, the fight is not fair.

"Let us cross, and we will face one another like honorable men," Olaf calls.

The English leader agrees. Convinced that his men can win, he cries, "A path is opened for you. Come quickly against us, men of war. God alone knows who will control the battlefield."

Then the battle began. A great cry went up. Hungry ravens and eagles circled overhead. Bows were busy, and shields caught sword points. Fighters fell on both sides, and young men lay on the field.

Then the battle began. A great cry went up. Hungry ravens and eagles circled overhead.

Olaf led us fearlessly, sword and spear in hand. After a long period of battle, a Viking wounded the aging English leader. Angered, the lord of the English thrust his knife into the proud Viking. The Englishman laughed and thanked his God for the day's work. His thanks were too soon. Another Viking threw a spear, bringing down the English leader. Still, he urged his men onward.

A young English lad, not fully grown, drew the spear from his master's chest and threw it back. The Viking who had killed the Englishman fell. So it continued, with good men falling on both sides, until our mighty warriors won the day.

My head is full of stories that I will tell upon our return home. Olaf has led his men to another great victory. Yet we must honor the courage of the English leader and his men. They would have made good Vikings!

QUESTIONS TO CONSIDER

1. Why were the Viking raiders able to conquer the British and other peoples? .

2. What was the highest good a Viking could have?

3. What do you think of the narrator's statement that "honorable Northmen do not steal. We gain only at the risk of our own lives"?

4. Many of the descriptions we have of the Vikings came from people they had conquered. How might this affect the accuracy of the descriptions?

Viking
by Susan M. Margeson

Susan M. Margeson gives an overview of the Vikings' way of life, presenting images of their furniture, clothing, weapons, jewelry, and many other items.

Norse Gods and Giants
by Ingri and Edgar Parin d'Aulaire

The d'Aulaires retell and illustrate the myths of the Norse gods and goddesses. These tales begin with the creation of the world and end with the final battle when the gods and giants destroy each other.

Sword Song
by Rosemary Sutcliff

Rosemary Sutcliff's historical novel tells the story of Bjarni, a young Viking, who is banished from his home for a killing he didn't intend. He becomes an outlaw, fighting for the clan chiefs on the west coast of Scotland.

Islam and Christianity

Muhammad
the Messenger

BY BARBARA LITTMAN

Muhammad ibn Abd Allah licked the last bit of pastry from his lips. The mixture of dates, walnuts, almonds, and honey had just the right amount of cinnamon and orange blossom flavor. The meal had been impressive—fresh yogurt, a spicy salad made with cracked wheat grains, roast goat and lamb, eggplant dumplings, spiced chickpeas and lentils, and goat's milk. His dear wife, Khadijah (kah•DEE•juh), had prepared a meal fit for kings, and his guests seemed well satisfied.

But no evening would be complete without poetry. **Arabs** were some of the best poets in the

---

People and Terms to Know

Muhammad (mu•HAM•ihd)—(c. 570–632) prophet and founder of Islam, the religion of the Muslims.

Arabs (AR•uhbs)—people of the large southwest Asian country of Arabia, where Muhammad was born.

Muhammad and his friend Abu Bakr hide in a cave to escape their enemies.
Note that Muhammad's face is covered. Devout Muslims do not make pictures

world. Arabs loved to write and listen to poetry. So of course, Muhammad had hired one of the best poets here in the city of **Mecca** to entertain his guests.

As the poet began to recite, Muhammad looked into the courtyard of his comfortable home. Fountains bubbled. Small birds bathed in the water. A breeze tickled the leaves of the dozen or so date-filled palm trees. Muhammad sighed. Inside, his home was just as beautiful. Colorful tiles brightened the walls. Brightly colored carpets and wall hangings made his home feel warm and comfortable. Candles and oil lamps cast flickering light across the rich colors and into the dark corners.

Muhammad sighed again. Even with all this, he was not content. Oh, he did not long for more beautiful things, more camels, or more gold. No, he was more than fortunate to have the worldly goods he did. For a poor orphan, taken in by an uncle after his parents' death, Muhammad had done very well. He was an honest, respected business-man who sold Arabian spices to the east.

People and Terms to Know

Mecca (MEH•kuh)—city in Arabia where Muhammad grew up. Mecca is a holy city for Muslim believers.

No, Muhammad was unhappy because he longed for the feelings he had had as a poor child. When he was a child, people cared about each other more. The needs of the tribe were more important than those of the individual. Now it seemed people cared more about themselves than about their tribe, and there was too much gambling and drinking.

"Muhammad, you are a messenger of God."

"Tomorrow I will return to my cave in the hills," thought Muhammad. For many years, Muhammad had been spending time alone in a cave on Mount Hira. There, he would meditate and think about how he could make life better.

The day after the dinner party, Muhammad set out for Mount Hira. The air smelled sweet with the odor of spices. The heat brought out the scent of plants where they grew on the dry hillsides. Here and there, Muhammad saw goats grazing on the thinly scattered grass.

When Muhammad arrived at the cave, it was dark and cool inside. He sat and thought for many hours. Then, to his surprise, he heard a voice. "Muhammad, you are a messenger of God," it said. It told him he must proclaim the word of God to his people.

Muhammad was uneasy. He was only forty years old, and he thought maybe he was going crazy. He decided to go home and tell his wife Khadijah what had happened. She thought God had sent the angel Gabriel to Muhammad to tell him he was a **prophet**. Khadijah believed Muhammad could be a good prophet who would help their people find a better way to live.

Khadijah told some of her friends and family about what had happened to Muhammad. They wanted to talk with him and find out what the angel had said. God also began to reveal more truths to Muhammad, who called these truths **revelations**.

Soon, more and more people were interested. Muhammad began to preach to small groups of people. Some people made fun of him, but many did not. They listened carefully and thought the revelations made sense. Later, people began to write them down. Eventually, all the revelations would be included in a book called the **Qur'an**.

People and Terms to Know

prophet (PRAH•fuht)—religious leader through whom the will of God is spoken.

revelations (REHV•uh•LAY•shuns)—truths that God revealed to the prophets. Muhammad's reports of his revelations form the basis for Islam.

Qur'an (kuh•RAN)—sacred text considered by Muslims to contain the revelations of God to Muhammad. It is sometimes spelled *Koran*.

Some people who listened to Muhammad's preaching were angry. These were merchants in Mecca who made a lot of money from people coming to pray at the **Ka'bah**. At this place, people worshipped many gods and goddesses. Muhammad said that people should worship only one God, Allah. The merchants were worried that people would stop coming to Mecca. If they did, the mer-

_____

Muhammad said that people should worship only one God, Allah.

_____

chants would not be rich anymore. They threatened Muhammad sometimes and even attacked him.

Muhammad and some of his followers decided they must leave Mecca. This was a sad time for Muhammad. Not only was he leaving his home, but his beloved wife Khadijah had died. They first went to the town of Ta'if, but soon the people there said they could not stay. Muhammad had to return to Mecca.

In Mecca, life became difficult. Muhammad and his followers heard a rumor that some people were planning to murder him. That night, Muhammad and a trusted friend, Abu Bakr, left the city

People and Terms to Know

Ka'bah (KAH•buh)—most sacred shrine in the Islamic world. It is toward the Ka'bah that Muslims turn when they pray.

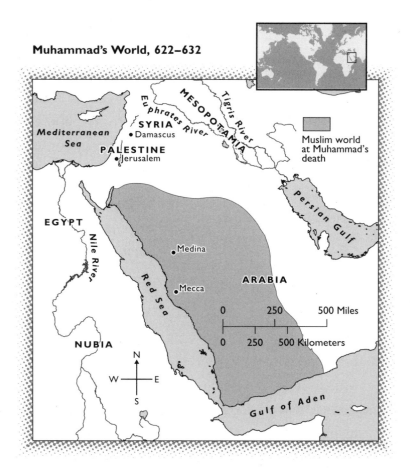

Muhammad's World, 622–632

Mediterranean Sea

Euphrates River

MESOPOTAMIA

Tigris River

SYRIA
• Damascus

PALESTINE
• Jerusalem

Muslim world at Muhammad's death

Persian Gulf

EGYPT

Nile River

Red Sea

• Medina

• Mecca

ARABIA

0   250   500 Miles

0   250   500 Kilometers

NUBIA

N
W — E
S

Gulf of Aden

and hid in a cave in the hills. Some people say the men who planned to kill Muhammad rode right by the cave but didn't look inside because a spider's web covered the opening. When it was safe to come out, the prophet and his friend went to Medina, a town where many of Muhammad's followers lived.

When Muhammad and Abu Bakr arrived in Medina, people were excited and happy. These **Muslims** were glad to see their prophet was safe. If his enemies had found Muhammad, they surely would have killed him. This important journey was called the **Hijrah**, and now marks the first year of the Muslim calendar.

Now Muhammad had a place to live where many people believed in his revelations. Muhammad still had a dream. He wanted to send the people who worshipped many gods and goddesses away and turn the Ka'bah into a place of worship for Muslims.

His opportunity came in 630. By this time, Muhammad had many followers. He decided it was time to march again on Mecca and try to take over the town. Muhammad and his men were well-armed and ready to fight.

When they got to Mecca, they were surprised. There was no one waiting to fight. A new leader had come to power in Mecca. He saw how many

---

People and Terms to Know

Muslims—people who accept Muhammad's teachings and follow the five pillars of a good Muslim life.

Hijrah (hih•JEE•ruh)—flight of Muhammad from Mecca to Medina in 622.

people were becoming Muslims. He also knew what good fighters Muhammad and his men were. He surrendered the city. Muhammad and his men entered the city peacefully.

Muhammad went straight to the Ka'bah. He touched the Black Stone at the eastern corner of the Ka'bah and shouted "Allahu Akbar," which means "God is great" in the Arabic language. From that moment forward, the Ka'bah became a Muslim shrine.

Muhammad returned to Medina in triumph. Everywhere Muslims rejoiced at Muhammad's great victory and looked forward to the time when they could make their own **pilgrimage** to Mecca.

* * *

Muhammad lived only two years after he took over the Ka'bah, but from the age of forty until he died, he founded an important new religion. Today, there are more than a billion Muslims. Twenty years after Muhammad's death, his revelations were written down in the Qur'an. The Qur'an also includes the five pillars of the Muslim religion.

People and Terms to Know

pilgrimage—journey to a sacred place or shrine.

1. Why did Muhammad want to find new ways to live?
2. Why do you think people were interested in hearing what Muhammad had to say?
3. What was Muhammad's message?
4. How would you describe Muhammad?

The Five Pillars of Islam

Faith A Muslim must publicly express belief in the following statement of faith: "There is no God but Allah, and Muhammad is the Messenger of Allah."

Prayer Five times a day, Muslims face toward the Ka'bah at Mecca to pray.

Alms All Muslims must help the poor by giving alms, or money for the poor, through a special religious tax.

Fasting During the Islamic holy month of Ramadan, Muslims must eat and drink nothing between sunrise and sunset. A simple meal is eaten at the end of the day.

Pilgrimage All Muslims must perform the hajj, or pilgrimage to Mecca, at least once in a lifetime.

Charlemagne and the Pope

BY STEPHEN CURRIE

Newspapers did not exist in the time of Charlemagne. But let's pretend one did.

The Frankish Post-Gazette

Before the printing press was invented

Son Born to King and Queen: Pope Sends Best Wishes

April 742—Last night Bertrada, Queen of the **Franks**, gave birth to a boy named Charles. Mother

---

People and Terms to Know

Franks—Germanic people whose territory, in Charlemagne's time, included some of present-day Germany, France, Belgium, and the Netherlands. Charlemagne was a Frank. The Franks had been Christians for several centuries by the time he was born.

Charlemagne is crowned emperor by Pope Leo III on Christmas Day in 800.

and child are said to be doing fine. Good wishes are pouring in from kings, lords, and bishops across Europe. Pope Zachary said he hopes the baby will grow up to be the second most powerful person in Europe, next to Zachary himself.

A spokesperson for King **Pepin the Short** described the baby as "incredibly cute," but a nurse, present at the birth, disagreed. "The kid is huge," she told our reporter. "He's already half the size of his father. Of course, with a dad called Pepin the Short, that's not difficult."

The Frankish Post-Gazette

Dedicated to corect speling of words

Pepin's Life Cut Short; Long Live New King(s)

September 768—The Frankish king Pepin the Short died yesterday after a short illness. Royal

---

People and Terms to Know

Pepin (PEHP•ihn) **the Short**—(c. 714–768) Charlemagne's father and king of the Franks (751–768). He helped Pope Stephen fight off an attack on Rome.

---

doctors did not release the cause of death. However, they say that poison has been ruled out. His kingdom will be divided between his sons, Charles—known as **Charlemagne**, or Charles the Great—and **Carloman**. Newly-elected Pope Stephen sent a message from Rome approving of the split.

The boundaries of the new kingdoms have not been determined, but most Franks have an opinion on the issue. In a survey taken by *Post-Gazette* staffers, 73 percent of adult Franks agreed with the statement, "I would prefer to be ruled by Charlemagne than by Carloman." "Carloman is an ordinary guy," said one woodworker, "but Charlemagne is emperor material. If I can't be in Charlemagne's territory, I quit."

People and Terms to Know

Charlemagne (SHAHR•luh•mayn)—(c. 741–814) king of the Franks from 768 to his death. He was crowned Roman Emperor of the West in 800. His name means "Charles the Great."

Carloman (CAHRL•uh•mahn)—(751–771) son of Pepin the Short. With his brother Charlemagne, he ruled the Franks until his death.

The Frankish Post-Gazette

Bringing the lastest news lately

Attacks Tax Saxons

December 772—Charlemagne has conquered the nearby **Saxons**. "All Saxony is now under the thumb of the Frankish king," reports a general. "Next we will overcome Bavaria and Lombardy."

"It was a great victory," says a soldier. "Charlemagne showed up covered in iron, with the sun's rays reflecting off the metal. The Saxons all ran in terror. It was cool."

Our loyal readers will recall that Charlemagne has ruled all of Frankland since the recent death (from natural causes; poison has been ruled out) of his brother Carloman. Charlemagne has begun expanding the borders of his kingdom. Perhaps he wants to become emperor—the first emperor in Western Europe since 476. "Great leaders need big territories," explains an aide. This guy is

---

People and Terms to Know

Saxons—Germanic people who were neighbors to the north and east of the Franks. Unlike the Franks, they were not Christians.

Charlemagne, right? Charles the Great—not Charles the Merely Okay."

In other news, Pope Stephen was replaced by Pope Adrian. Details were unavailable at press time.

The Frankish Post-Gazette

Charlemagne to Pope: Who's Number One?

April 774—Frankland is bigger than ever. Charlemagne's armies have nearly reached to Rome. Last night, Pope Adrian met with Charlemagne and asked for some of the king's lands. "Adrian thinks popes should have more power," explained one of Adrian's assistants. "The pope should be Number One, but kings don't take him seriously any more. Extra land would help. Charlemagne has plenty of land—why not share?"

Charlemagne refused. "Turning the pope down suggests that Charlemagne wants to be emperor, not just king," said one scholar. "He wants to run

▲

This silver sculpture of Charlemagne contained a piece
of the emperor's skull.

the government and the Church." Charlemagne,
however, had no comment. "We won this territory
through hard work," points out a general. "We
used soldiers, weapons, and armor. If the pope
wants more land, maybe he should get an iron suit
like the one Charlemagne wears."

The Frankish
Post-Gazette

Today's news is tomorrow's history

New Pope Chosen: Charlemagne Gives Him Half a Thumb Up

December 795—Following the unexpected death of Pope Adrian (from natural causes; poison has been ruled out), bishops in Rome have chosen a new leader for the Church. **Pope Leo III** is set to take office next week. But, there's a difference of opinion about the choice. Some have accused Leo of immoral behavior in the past. Charlemagne's public relations officer reported the king's reaction to the change in popes: "He's sorry to lose Adrian; they were good friends. As for Leo? Well, he was the best man available."

People and Terms to Know

Pope Leo III—pope from 795 to 816. His enemies accused him of selling Church jobs to the highest bidder and of other immoral behaviors. He was attacked by his enemies in 799.

The Frankish Post-Gazette

Charlemagne Rescues Pope from Angry Mob; Leo Grateful

May 799—Last month Pope Leo was savagely attacked on the streets of Rome. A mob with knives beat him and tried to cut out his eyes. "It was awful," said a Roman who saw the events. "Of course, Leo had it coming, with all that immoral behavior." Leo escaped, but staying in Rome was out of the question. "Too dangerous," said an aide. "His enemies are everywhere."

So, the pope sent a message to Charlemagne, begging for help. According to a palace source, Charlemagne has decided to send troops to Rome to attack Leo's enemies. "We don't expect a reward," said the source, "but if the pope feels like doing something nice for Charlemagne in return, we can think of a few possibilities."

The Frankish Post-Gazette

King Made Emperor as Thousands Cheer

December 800—Just call him Emperor Charlemagne. Last year, loyal readers will recall, Charlemagne rescued Pope Leo from a mob of angry Romans and sent troops to wipe out Leo's enemies. Yesterday, it was payback time. Leo formally crowned Charlemagne the first **Western Roman Emperor** in more than three centuries.

The mood in Rome, where the ceremony took place, was joyful and enthusiastic. "We always knew Charlemagne was the greatest," said a citizen. Charlemagne wore a long tunic with a golden belt and jeweled sandals. At the high point of the ceremony, Leo placed a golden crown on Charlemagne's head. Then Pope Leo lay on the floor and kissed the hem of Charlemagne's cloak.

People and Terms to Know

Western Roman Emperor—ruler of the western part of the old Roman Empire. The Roman Empire had first been split into eastern and western halves around 286. The last Western emperor had to step down in 476.

The ceremony proved that Charlemagne is now more powerful than the pope, experts agree. As Western Roman Emperor, Charlemagne leads both Church and government. "Charlemagne's Number One," said one. "Leo's now Number Two." Predicted one person who watched, "This Roman Empire idea will probably catch on. I wouldn't be surprised if we had Roman emperors running around for the next thousand years or so."

QUESTIONS TO CONSIDER

1. Why do you think Pepin the Short divided his kingdom equally between his two sons before he died? What might have been the advantages and disadvantages of doing this?

2. Why do you think Charlemagne agreed to help Pope Leo, even though he had been lukewarm about Leo's election as pope?

3. What do you think is the importance of Pope Leo kissing the hem of Charlemagne's cloak?

4. What do you think is the importance of Charlemagne taking the title of Western Roman Emperor?

Frankish Annals

Instead of newspapers, people in the middle ages used annals to report important events. Annals are year-by-year historical records. The following entry from one of the annals of the Franks records the coronation of Charlemagne's father, Pepin the Short.

751. In this year Pepin was named king of the Franks with the sanction of the pope, and in the city of Soissons he was anointed with the holy oil by the hands of Boniface, archbishop and martyr of blessed memory, and was raised to the throne after the custom of the Franks. But Childerich, who had the name of king, was shorn of his locks and sent into a monastery.

The World in the Time of Charlemagne
by Fiona Macdonald

Fiona Macdonald presents the history of Charlemagne's life and reign and describes what was happening in the rest of the world during this period.

His Majesty's Elephant
by Judith Tarr

Judith Tarr uses the court of Charlemagne as the background for a tale of fantasy. In this story, two young people battle evil forces that are threatening the emperor and his realm.

Legends of Charlemagne
by Thomas Bulfinch

Thomas Bulfinch's classic retelling presents the famous medieval tales of Roland and the other great warriors of Charlemagne's court.

Avicenna, Prince of Philosophy

BY WALTER HAZEN

My friend Silvio and I are always arguing. Our teachers say we would rather argue than eat. But we are university students. Students are supposed to argue. Right?

Silvio and I are students at the University of Salerno in southern Italy. Salerno is a medical school, and we are studying to become doctors. I enrolled two years ago, in 1237. Silvio entered just recently. He is from the North, but I forgive him for that.

Recently, Silvio has been in no mood to argue. He says he doesn't feel well and that he has no energy. He thinks he has some terrible disease. He eats little and sleeps even less. He wonders if he is being punished for something he has done.

شفامی دهذکه معاودت صوف بنذذ ۰ ومن یحکم این مقدمات ازعلم طب تبرا

An Arab doctor examines his patient

"Nonsense!" I said to him one day. "The only thing wrong with you is that you have a bad case of love sickness."

"Love what?" he responded. He looked at me as if I had a hole in my head.

"Love sickness," I said again. "Have you not heard of **Avicenna**, the great Arab doctor? Of course not; you have only recently arrived. You have not been introduced to his wonderful medical book. It explains all sorts of things that people in the West find absolutely amazing."

I went on to explain that Avicenna was the first doctor to discuss how the mind can influence one's health. He talked about love sickness and how it can actually make a person physically ill. I should explain that Silvio recently met a girl named Maria, the daughter of one of our teachers. It was clear to me from the start—we Southerners are wise in the ways of love—that Silvio liked her a lot.

People and Terms to Know

Avicenna (AV•ih•SEHN•uh)—(980–1037) Arab doctor and philosopher, born in Bukhara, a city in central Asia. His medical book, the *Canon of Medicine*, was used in Europe until the 1600s. He is believed to have written around 200 works.

I told Silvio that since Maria was unaware of his feelings and because he was too shy to approach her, his situation had made him sick. What did Avicenna recommend that a love-struck gentleman do? Why, go to the girl and let her know his feelings. Then— and only then—would the signs of sickness disappear.

What did Avicenna recommend that a love-struck gentleman do?

Silvio wanted to know more about Avicenna. Until he enrolled at Salerno, he had always considered **Galen** the greatest doctor from the past. Now his eyes widened as I continued to tell him more about this famous Arab doctor.

Silvio was especially interested in Avicenna's youth. He shook his head in disbelief when I told him that Avicenna had a great mind even as a child.

"Come on, Guido," he objected. "No ten-year-old child could remember the entire Qur'an word for word. I find that hard to believe."

People and Terms to Know

Galen (GAY•luhn)—(c. 130–c. 200) Greek doctor and writer.

I told him that not only could Avicenna recite the Muslim holy book from cover to cover, he taught himself medicine by the time he was thirteen. I further pointed out that when he was sixteen, Avicenna cured the **emir** of Bukhara of an illness that well-known doctors at the time could not treat. After that, his fame grew, and Avicenna found his way into the courts of a number of Arab rulers.

I went on to tell Silvio that Avicenna was known in his day as "The Prince of Philosophers."

"I know," Silvio said, "that a philosopher is someone who studies and searches for the truth about life. At least you don't have to explain *that*. What else did he do?"

"Well, he knew about mathematics, geology, and music. He was a government official for a time, and he wrote about metaphysics," I said.

"That, or those, I don't know much about," Silvio said, frowning.

"Metaphysics is a branch of philosophy. It's the study of the nature of the universe," I said. "And I forgot to mention that he even found time to write some poetry."

People and Terms to Know

emir (ih•MIHR)—prince or chieftain in the Middle East.

"So when did he have time to write about medicine?" asked Silvio, yawning.

"Good question," I said. "Maybe he didn't sleep much either."

Our interest in Avicenna, of course, is limited to medicine. I explained to Silvio that the word *canon* as used in the title of Avicenna's book means "a list." That is what the book is: a list of all the medical knowledge passed on by the Greeks and the Romans and added to by Avicenna and other Arab physicians.

▲

An Arabic medical text identifies plants that can heal.

Silvio was surprised to learn that Avicenna's book discussed removing cataracts from eyes.

"I know about cataracts," he said. "They start with a cloudy film in the eye and can cause blindness."

"Right," I said. "He also wrote about stitching wounds with animal gut. And he listed 760 drugs for healing."

Silvio whistled in surprise. "If I live to be a hundred and fifty, I could never imagine that many drugs. That is unbelievable," he said.

Silvio was even more surprised when I told him about some of Avicenna's advanced ideas. One of these was that certain diseases can be spread by water and soil.

"That is truly amazing," Silvio commented. "And here in Europe people are still blaming sickness on evil spirits and other such foolishness."

Silvio and I have had many discussions about Avicenna since that early conversation. Also, I should point out that he took the great doctor's advice and told Maria of his feelings. To his complete surprise, she did not laugh at him. They see each other quite a lot. Maybe they will be married someday. Oh, yes— Silvio is eating and sleeping normally again. And he is arguing just as strongly as ever!

QUESTIONS TO CONSIDER

1. What do you think about Avicenna's ideas about the relationship between emotions, such as love, and illness?

2. How do you think people today would react to Avicenna's idea that certain diseases can be spread by soil and water?

3. How did medical knowledge in Europe compare with that of the Arab world at the same time?

Saints and
Sinners

Bad King John

BY STEPHEN FEINSTEIN

Big gray clouds drifted overhead. There was a promise of rain in the cool wind off the North Sea. My little grandson Gavin was walking beside me across the fields of my Yorkshire estate. We passed my tenants hard at work in the fields, **serfs** and freemen alike. We stopped to watch them for a while. The men were cutting the wheat with their sickles, which had sharp, curved blades, while the women gathered the cut wheat.

Old William, sickle in hand, looked up from his work and greeted us. "Good day, my lord," he called. "And how goes the young Master Gavin?"

People and Terms to Know

serfs—workers who could not legally leave the estate of the lord they worked for.

King John receives the gift of a cup from a petitioner asking for a favor.

"Will," I said, "we must get the harvest in before the rains begin in earnest."

"Aye, sir, that we must," said William. "At least we don't have to worry about the king taking our land and crops like in the days of King **John**."

"May we never have such a bad king again," I said.

A vivid image of King John's face flashed before me.

William turned back to his work, and we walked on. I felt a few drops and then many more. I glanced up at the sky and prayed that the rain would be brief and not ruin the harvest.

"Gavin, let's make a run for those trees over there," I cried, pointing to the edge of the meadow. We sat on a large rock under a huge old oak. "We'll stay dry here until the rain stops."

"Grandpa, why was King John a bad king?" Gavin asked. "Did you know him?"

"I met King John a few times," I said.

"Well, why don't you like him?" Gavin said.

A vivid image of King John's face flashed before me—his lips curled in his typical sneer of contempt,

People and Terms to Know

John—(1167–1216) king of England from 1199 to 1216. He was the son of Henry II and Eleanor of Aquitaine. English nobles forced King John to sign the Magna Carta, the most important document in English constitutional history.

his eyes filled with suspicion. "Gavin my boy, it's a long story," I said. I began with a sigh. "King **Henry II** and his wife **Eleanor of Aquitaine** had five sons. The youngest was called John Lackland."

Gavin laughed. "What a funny name!"

"Well, John didn't think it was funny," I said. "He was called by this nickname because he wasn't going to get any land when his father died. But he wanted land—in fact, he wanted to be king! By the time King Henry died, his two eldest sons had also died. So Richard, who was older than John, became the next king."

"Was Richard a good king?" asked Gavin.

"He was a brave warrior, and he loved to fight. We called him **Richard the Lion-Hearted**. He looked a bit like a lion, with his mane of red-gold hair. But was he a good king? We never had much chance to find out. Just two months after his coronation, King Richard and his knights set off on one of the **Crusades**

People and Terms to Know

Henry II—(1133–1189) king of England (1154–1189). A strong king who expanded England's territory in Wales and Ireland, he is best known for expressing his shame publicly after some of his knights murdered Archbishop Thomas à Becket, with whom he had quarreled.

Eleanor of Aquitaine (AK•wih•TAYN)—(c. 1122–1204) queen of France (1137–1152) and queen of England (1152–1204).

Richard the Lion-Hearted—(1157–1199) king of England from 1189 to 1199.

Crusades—military expeditions undertaken by Christian powers to win the Holy Land from the Muslims. There were Crusades in the 1000s, 1100s, and 1200s.

to free the Holy Land. We did not see him again for about four years. Before he went away, Richard gave large estates of land to his little brother, Prince John."

"John must have been happy to get the land," said Gavin.

"Not exactly," I said. "You see, John always wanted more—more land, more money, more power. After three years of fighting in the Holy Land, Richard decided to return to England. On his way home, he was captured by Duke Leopold of Austria. Word reached England that Richard was being held prisoner. But John announced that Richard had been killed, and he declared himself king."

"John always wanted more— more land, more money, more power."

"So that's how he repaid his brother's kindness," Gavin said. "Is that the reason you don't like him?"

"There were many reasons," I said. "Anyway, those of us who knew that Richard was alive paid a huge sum of money to Leopold to set him free. Richard finally did return home, but he left within a month, never to set foot in England again."

"Did he punish his brother John before he went away again?" asked Gavin.

"Amazingly, Richard forgave him. Richard really didn't want to be king. He preferred being a soldier," I said. "Richard spent the next five years fighting in France, and he took back lands he had lost to the French king. You see, parts of the English kingdom lie across the English Channel in France. One day, during a minor battle, an arrow struck Richard in the shoulder. Before he died, he named his brother John as king."

"What did people think about that?" said Gavin.

"The people of England and Normandy, a region across the channel, accepted John. Those in other regions in France did not," I answered. "They wanted John's young nephew, Arthur, to be their king. Of course, John was not happy about this."

A sudden gust of wind blew cold rain into our faces. I tightened Gavin's cloak about him.

"So what happened to Arthur?" Gavin went on. "Did something bad happen?"

"I'm afraid so," I said. "He disappeared. People say that John had Arthur murdered. We don't know for sure. Young Arthur was never seen or heard from again.

Over the next few years, King John fought a losing war in France against the French king. Finally, John returned to England. He had lost all the French lands that Richard had won. Behind his back, people began to call the king John Softsword."

"What did John do when he got back to England?" asked Gavin.

"The king was determined to get his lands back from the French," I said, "and he needed lots of money to do it. So he raised taxes on all of us, rich and poor alike. He seemed ready to make us all penniless."

"Did you have to give him anything?" said Gavin.

"Indeed I did," I said. "One day King John and his knights appeared at our house. We had to provide food and beds. Then he demanded that we give him part of our harvest. He also wanted all of our gold and jewels or he would take our land. We had no choice but to obey. He had made similar threats to our neighbors. He arrested people and had them tortured, or even killed, if they did not obey him. He even managed to offend the Church."

"So John really was a bad king," said Gavin.

"Very bad," I said. "Finally, we got fed up with the tyrant. I joined forces with other barons. (A baron has land given by the king.) Together, we drew up a list of demands. We were determined to limit the king's power for our own protection.

"We sent word to the king that unless he signed the document, the whole country would rise up against him. I suppose he knew when he was beaten. I'll never forget the day we met him at **Runnymede**. King John was furious. He smiled a false and evil little smile as he fixed his royal seal on the document that came to be called the **Magna Carta**. For the first time, England knew that the king is not above the law, English subjects have rights, and nobody shall be denied justice."

"Did King John live up to his agreement?" asked Gavin.

"Not likely," I said, shaking my head. "John refused to change his ways. By September, we had a civil war in England. The following year, John

---

People and Terms to Know

Runnymede (RUHN•nee•meed)—meadow west of London on the south bank of the Thames River where the Magna Carta was signed in 1215.

Magna Carta (MAG•nuh KAHR•tuh)—Latin for "Great Charter." It is the basis for our modern system of justice. Among other things, it granted the right to a trial by jury and established that the law was more important than the king.

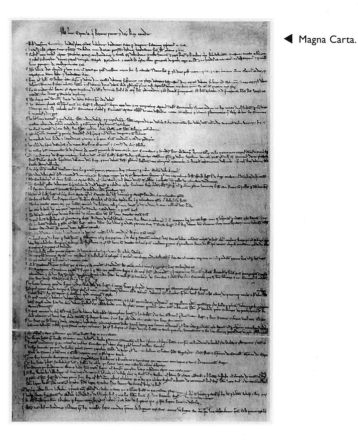

◀ Magna Carta.

was marching through rebel territory. His men burned villages, torturing and killing English subjects.

"In the end, the king got what was coming to him. As John and his men crossed an inlet of the North Sea on the east coast, his royal treasure chest was washed away! John became ill. He died a few days later at a nearby castle. So King John was bad till the end."

The rain had stopped, and the sun sparkled through the wet leaves.

"Tell me more about the lost treasure, Grandpa," said Gavin.

"That's a story for another day," I said.

QUESTIONS TO CONSIDER

1. How did John, the youngest son of Henry II, get to be king?
2. How did John betray Richard when Richard was captured and held prisoner?
3. Why did the English barons demand that King John sign the Magna Carta?
4. What does this story show about the power of the English king in the 1200s?

The Merry Adventures of Robin Hood
by Howard Pyle

King John's great legendary foes were the outlaws of Sherwood Forest, who "rob from the rich and give to the poor." Howard Pyle's version of the tales of Robin Hood and his archenemy, the Sheriff of Nottingham, is a classic.

The Crusader King: Richard the Lion-Hearted
by Richard Suskind

John's brother, King Richard the Lion-Hearted, spent only six months of his ten-year reign in England. Richard Suskind's biography gives an account of the king's adventurous life.

Proud Taste for Scarlet and Miniver
by E. L. Konigsburg

E. L. Konigsburg's historical novel tells the story of King John's mother, Eleanor of Acquitaine. The brilliant and beautiful Eleanor was first queen of France and then queen of England.

St. Thomas Aquinas Kidnapped

BY LYNNETTE BRENT

Paris
August 28, 1243

My dear sister Teresa,

Thank you for your letter. I have so much work to do here at the **order**, and I sometimes feel over-whelmed. It was wonderful to get your good news. I could almost see the fat grapes ripening in the warm sun of home. I wish that things were going so smoothly here. We are having great difficulty with a new student who is set to join us.

People and Terms to Know

order—group of religious persons, such as monks, living together. The letter-writer is a friar of the Dominican Order.

Thomas Aquinas must have studied in a classroom much like this one in a university of the Middle Ages.

The student—**Thomas Aquinas**—is not the problem himself. He was a student at the University of Naples, and he has a reputation for being quite bright and for studying very hard. He should have no trouble with the program our founder Dominic set up for all who want to join the order. As I did, he will attend lectures on **theology**, learn the Bible and the traditions and history of the Church, and participate in discussions with teachers and fellow students. This is how we prepare our minds and hearts for our way of life.

The problem with Thomas is not that he is unprepared to join us here. The problem is that his family disapproves of his plans. They want him to have a religious life, but not in our humble order. They were hoping that he would become a member of the Benedictine Order and quickly rise to be head of the monastery at Monte Cassino. So now Thomas's mother is trying to talk him out of joining us.

People and Terms to Know

Thomas Aquinas (uh•KWY•nuhs)—(1225–1274) Italian student at the time of this story. Later he became the greatest philosopher and scholar of the medieval Church. He wrote *Summa Theologica*. In 1323, the Church declared him a saint.

theology (thee•AWL•uh•jee)—study of religious faith and experience, especially the study of God and God's relationship to the world.

We do have a plan for helping Thomas. We are going to send him to Rome for a brief time. Then he will travel to Paris, or perhaps Cologne, Germany, where he will be able to begin his studies.

Are these extreme measures? Yes, sister, I suppose that they are. But Thomas's family is powerful and wealthy—he was born in a castle in southern Italy! We feel that we need to help him in some way.

I pray that you continue to be well. I will let you know what happens to my new friend.

Your devoted brother,
Andrew

September 15, 1243

Dear Thomas,

I hope my letter finds you well. I was glad when we got word that your mother would allow us to write to you. I will continue to write to you every week until you are no longer a prisoner.

We were deeply saddened when we learned that you were kidnapped when you left Naples. Of course we knew that your family disapproved of your plan to join the order, but we never expected that your brothers would take you prisoner. How lonely you must be, locked up in a tower of your own home. I trust you are being well fed! We have heard that even your mother is saddened by this extreme turn of events. It's too bad that her wish to keep you from being a poor monk forced her to treat you like a criminal.

> How lonely you must be, locked up in a tower of your own home.

She has allowed us to contact you, though. I'm hoping this means that she will soon decide to set you free.

We are also planning to ask the pope to help you. Your family has supported the pope and the Church in the past. We hope that a plea from someone in such a powerful position will make your release come more quickly. We are doing all we can.

You will hear from me again soon.
Friar Andrew

March 18, 1244

My Friend,

I am so sorry that you are still in your tower. We continue to ask the pope to aid you. We are seeking help from your uncle at the court of Emperor **Frederick II**, especially since your brothers are soldiers in the emperor's army.

In your last letter to me, you said that your family continues to try to destroy your will to become a priest in the Dominican Order. You should be very proud of the way you have resisted them. God be praised for your strength! We are looking forward to having you join us.

Stay strong, brother Thomas. I know that your faith will help you. We are all praying that your family will see how important it is for you to join us and continue your religious studies. I hope you are reading your Bible every day. We pray for you.

Your friend,
Friar Andrew

November 21, 1244

Most humble Thomas,

I am happy that you have remained strong even as you are struggling with your family. Your sister seems to be softening her harsh opinion of your

---

People and Terms to Know

Frederick II—(1194–1250) Holy Roman emperor from 1220 to 1250; great patron of artists and thinkers.

decision. She was kind to provide you with a copy of the Bible, as well as writings from other scholars. You have spent your time in prison well. I am interested in the ideas about religion and science that you explained in your last letter.

For many years, the Church has taught that all good and worthwhile thoughts come from prayer and the Bible alone. Many men of science have been punished for their ideas—ideas that didn't come directly from the study of religion. Yet you wrote that science and religion do not have to conflict. You say that God gave

Many men of science have been punished for their ideas.

people the gift of reasoning. If people use this gift, along with prayer and studying religious writings, then scientific ideas do not need to go against what the Church teaches. Some things can be experienced through the senses, and some things must be learned through prayer. Do I understand this correctly? If so, you could completely change ideas about science and religious thought! Oh, how I wish that you were free to study and debate with us in Paris!

When you are able to come, bring warm clothes. The winter rains have started, and the city is gray and cold.

I continue to pray for your release,
Friar Andrew

February 2, 1245

Dear Teresa,

I have exciting, hopeful news! Both the emperor and the pope have agreed to try to persuade Thomas's family to change their minds. I can't imagine that any family would go against both the emperor and the pope! (To tell the truth, the emperor and the pope are not on good terms just now, but that is another story.)

The Dominicans have contacted Thomas's mother in hopes that she is finally ready to set Thomas free. A group of friars will be waiting at the family castle for her decision. I was asked to join them! I look forward to meeting my dear friend face-to-face for the first time. I can't wait to tell you all the details of our first meeting.

Thomas's ideas are different from the ideas we have held in the past. I'm certain that he will soon have a place among the best scholars in the Church.

Thank you, Teresa, for your kind support throughout these times. I will let you know what happens next.

Your hopeful Brother,
Friar Andrew

QUESTIONS TO CONSIDER

1. What events led to Thomas's kidnapping?
2. How did Thomas spend his time after he was kidnapped?
3. How would you describe Friar Andrew?
4. What does this story tell you about the role of religion in medieval life?
5. Why do you think Thomas Aquinas is important to world history?

The Pardoner's Tale

BY STEPHEN CURRIE, RETOLD FROM
GEOFFREY CHAUCER'S *CANTERBURY TALES*

"The greatest sin of all," the **Pardoner** said, "is the sin of greed."

The Pardoner looked around at the men and women sitting by the fireside. All of them were **pilgrims** heading toward **Canterbury**, just like the Pardoner himself. They had stopped for the night at an inn south of London. His eye caught each person in turn—the Knight, the Monk, the Friar, the Clerk.

People and Terms to Know

Pardoner (PAHR•duhn•uhr)—in the Middle Ages, a church official. He raised money for religious works by asking for money when he forgave, or pardoned, people for their sins. In Geoffrey Chaucer's *The Canterbury Tales*, written in the 1300s, a pardoner is one of a group of people on the way to Canterbury.

pilgrims—people who go on a journey to a religious place, such as Canterbury.

Canterbury (KAN•tuhr•BEHR•ee)—town in southern England. In the cathedral, or large church, at Canterbury is the tomb of Saint Thomas à Becket. He had been a high official in the Church who had been murdered there. The tomb attracted many pilgrims.

The Pardoner carrying one of his relics. (See note on page 124.)

Throughout the evening they had taken turns telling tales, and now at last it was the Pardoner's chance.

The flames sparked and danced in the darkness, and a small smile spread across the Pardoner's lips. He had been waiting for this moment.

"The greatest of all evils is greed. Look!" He reached inside his cloak and pulled out a sheep's bone. "Here is a magic bone! A holy **relic** from a holy sheep. Dip the bone in any well, and the well water will take on magical healing powers." The Pardoner's voice moved into a familiar sing-song. How many times had he spoken those exact words? He had certainly said them often enough to have them completely memorized, anyway.

It was working, just as it always did. Even now, in the late 1300s, people still wanted to believe that what he said was true. His audience leaned forward, curious. The Pardoner raised his voice slightly, to draw in even those in the back. "If your sick cow drinks the water, she will recover. The same is true for your dying horse. Even your jealous husband will no longer be jealous once he drinks from a well touched by this bone!" He waited for the laugh,

---

People and Terms to Know

relic (REHL•ihk)—part of the body or object belonging to a holy person and kept as something to be honored. The Pardoner's "relics" were not like that.

which came quickly. "Like it?" he added. "I rent it out—cheap!"

The Pardoner set the bone carefully on the floor in front of him and reached back into his cloak. "Look! A magic mitten!" With a flourish, he drew out an ordinary-looking mitten. "Put your hand inside this mitten, this holy relic, and it will make you rich beyond your wildest dreams! It will give you the magic touch, my friends. Your land will give twice the crops it used to. Three times, even!" With one hand he tossed the mitten up into the air. With the other hand he plucked it out of the air in one quick motion. "A magic mitten!" he repeated. "It's for rent—cheap!"

"How much?" someone called.

The Pardoner set the mitten on the floor next to the bone. Should he try to sell them? No, he decided, and he straightened up, shaking his head. Making another sale right now was tempting, but telling a good story to this audience was even better. "You really don't want them," he admitted. "These relics have no value at all." He picked the bone up and tossed it casually over his shoulder. "It's ordinary. I bought it from a butcher for a few pennies. The mitten won't do a thing to help your crops. The only person who gets rich off these so-called magical relics is me!"

"How do you do that?" the Knight challenged him.

"I travel from town to town, as you know," the Pardoner explained. "I preach, and I offer the people who listen pardons for their bad behavior—that's why they call me a Pardoner, after all. I forgive the people their sins. Of course, I make them pay first. I charge them to touch the bone and to put their hand in the mitten. The more they pay, the more sins I pardon. Oh, don't look so shocked—that's exactly what I do! And I make a very comfortable living." He smiled, and his long, shiny hair gleamed in the firelight. "I don't really take anybody's sins away, you know, but I do one very good work—line my pockets with the people's gold."

"I forgive the people their sins. Of course, I make them pay first."

The Merchant stood. "I see," he remarked slowly, and he stared at the Pardoner's face. "Greed is the worst sin of all, you say, and yet you are perhaps the greediest."

"I live for greed," the Pardoner said proudly. "And I live on it, too—the greed of those who want more wealth, the greed of those who want instant pardon for their sins. But listen!" he commanded, and his voice rang out across the fire. Those who had begun to whisper to each other stopped and looked up. "I am not the greediest of all. Listen to my tale, and you shall see who is."

"Tell us," said the Plowman, and the rest of the company sat back and nodded.

"Once," began the Pardoner, "there were three young men who spent their days engaged in sin." His voice sounded as if he disapproved. "They danced, they drank, they swore, they did all kinds of bad things. They made merry from the afternoon until early in the morning.

"Sinners often come to bad ends," the Pardoner said in a sad voice, although he liked wine as well as anybody and was proud of having girlfriends in several towns. "Certainly these three young men were far too merry for their own good."

"What happened?" asked one of the nuns.

"A plague struck," said the Pardoner, "and many of their friends died of the disease. In a rage, the three decided to end their drinking and their chasing girls. Instead, they agreed, they would find Death himself and challenge him to combat. For if Death killed their friends, they said, then he had to be killed himself."

"Makes sense to me," murmured the Miller.

"And so they asked an old man they met if he knew where Death was," the Pardoner continued. He dropped another log on the fire, which flared up suddenly. "'Death?' the old man said." The Pardoner imitated the cracked voice of an elderly man. The Knight and the Clerk smiled. "'Why, I've been looking for him for months!' He was an old man, and he wished to die," the Pardoner explained.

"Did the three hurt the old man?" asked the Knight, his hand moving to grasp his sword.

"N o," said the Pardoner, "but they threatened him, even though they knew they must always show respect to old people. And finally he told them where he had last seen Death. 'Behind that oak tree over there—'" Slowly, the Pardoner stretched out his finger and pointed across the fire the way he imagined the old man must have done.

"So the three men rushed to the tree," the **Wife of Bath** said impatiently. "And?"

People and Terms to Know

Wife of Bath—character in Chaucer's *Canterbury Tales*, she was a married woman from the town of Bath in southwest England.

"And what did they find there?" the Pardoner asked. "The did not find Death. He was gone. But there was something else. Money! Eight bushels of coins if there was an ounce. And the three greedy young men threw themselves upon it. Why, ·there was enough money to last them the rest of their lives. There was only one problem—" He paused.

"It wasn't theirs," said the Priest, sadly shaking his head.

"That's right," said the Pardoner, "and that meant trouble. They couldn't carry it out of the woods just as it was. People would ask questions. 'Where'd you get those coins?' 'Hey, that looks like my money!' So they decided to carry it out by night."

The wind picked up. A few sparks rose up from the fire and danced crazily up the chimney. The two nuns huddled closer together.

"So they stayed all day?" asked the Parson. "They wouldn't dare leave, would they? For fear someone else would find the treasure and rob Death instead."

"But they'd get hungry," the Miller objected.

"They would." The Pardoner nodded. "And they did. So they decided to send one of them to town to buy food and drinks for the all of them. They drew straws, just like we did tonight to see in what order we would tell our tales. The youngest of the three drew the shortest straw, and he went off to the town."

"And?" the Monk prompted.

"While he was gone," the Pardoner said, "the other two put their heads together. Splitting the treasure into three parts would have been enough for any of us. But it wasn't enough for them. 'Why should we split it three ways when we can split it two?' one asked the other. So they plotted to kill their friend when he came back. Each would take a dagger and stab him the moment he arrived."

The Priest made a face and pulled his cloak tightly around himself. "No details, please," he said.

The Pardoner shrugged. "But in the meantime the man who had gone to town decided that one third of the treasure wasn't enough for him either. While in town, he bought three bottles of wine. He also bought poison—strong, fast-acting poison— and dropped some into two of the bottles. Then he went back and——"

"I see." One of the nuns shuddered. "The two who stayed behind threw themselves upon him and killed him."

"That's right," the Pardoner said, smiling broadly. "And immediately after that they—"

"They drank the bottles of wine," interrupted the Clerk. "They drank the poisoned bottles. And then they died, too."

"Right again," said the Pardoner. "So, you see, they found Death after all. It was greed that led them there, for greed is the greatest of all evils." He stooped over and picked up the bone and the mitten from the floor. "Speaking of greed, by the way, anyone want to touch a magical relic?"

QUESTIONS TO CONSIDER

1. What is odd about the Pardoner saying that greed is the greatest of sins?

2. What does the pilgrims' interest in relics tell you about life in the 1300s?

3. Why do you think the word Death is capitalized in the story? What does this have to do with the way people in the Middle Ages might have thought about death?

4. Why do you think people were so easily fooled by the Pardoner? What are some ways people are easily fooled today?

The Canterbury Tales
Retold by Geraldine McCaughrean

Geraldine McCaughrean presents modern retellings of a number of the best known of Geoffrey Chaucer's Canterbury Tales.

The Challenge of the Green Knight
by Ian Seraillier

The other great English writer of Geoffrey Chaucer's time was the author of Sir Gawain and the Green Knight. Ian Seraillier creates a modern version of this wonder tale of King Arthur's court.

The Ramsay Scallop
by Frances Temple

Frances Temple's historical novel describes the adventures of a young man and woman on a pilgrimage during the Middle Ages.

The Maid
of Orléans

BY MARIANNE McCOMB

This is a record of the final hours of **Joan of Arc**,
the Maid of **Orléans**. Some have called her a witch
and a **heretic**, but I call her a hero and a saint.
I believe in my heart that she alone saved France
and did so with the help of God.

Know this about me: I speak only the truth.
I am a priest at the prison in Rouen (roo•AHN),
which is a city in northern France. I was sent to
pray with Joan on the last night of her life. When I
was led into her dark cell, the poor girl fell to her

People and Terms to Know

Joan of Arc—(c. 1412–1431) French peasant girl who led a successful
defeat of the English at Orléans in 1429.

Orléans (awr•lay•AHN)—city of north-central France.

heretic (HEHR•ih•tihk)—person who disagrees with the established
beliefs of a church. The opinion of that person is called heresy
(HEHR•ih•see).

Joan of Arc in armor with her banner showing St. Michael, St. Margaret, and St. Catherine.

knees. She was afraid to die, she said, and was in need of comfort. But what comfort could I give this frightened girl?

Outside, we could hear the jailers putting up a stake on a high platform in the market square. Townspeople hurried back and forth gathering wood for the fire. Joan was to be burned at the stake in the morning.

All through that long night, I sat with Joan. It calmed her to speak, so I asked her to tell me her story. Although she trembled like a leaf, her voice was strong and sure. This is the story she told me.

Joan was born in Domrémy, a small village in eastern France. She was the daughter of poor peasants. One day, when Joan was thirteen years old, she heard a voice call her name. She looked up and saw a great light shining on her. In the center of the light was Saint Michael, the warrior archangel who commands all God's armies of angels.

Michael spoke to Joan in simple language so that she could understand. He told her to be good and to say her prayers every night. Then he told her the story of King **Charles VII** of France, who was

---

People and Terms to Know

Charles VII—(1403–1461) king of France. He fought England for the right to rule. With the help of Joan of Arc, he was crowned in 1429, and ruled until his death.

in great danger. For years now, the English had occupied much of northern France. Charles VII, who was the rightful heir to the throne, had never been crowned because Reims (reemz), the city in northern France where French kings are crowned, lay within English territory.

Michael said that God wanted Joan to take Charles to Reims to be crowned king. When Joan said that the job was impossible for a poor peasant girl, Saint Michael said, "God will help you. Be ready, and He will show you how to save France."

In the months following Saint Michael's visit, Joan was visited by two other saints, Saint Catherine and Saint Margaret. Both had the same message for her: "Be good, and wait to hear from us."

Then, in 1428, the saints came to Joan and told her that they wanted her to save Orléans. For more than a year, Orléans had been surrounded by the English. The saints said Joan should drive the English out of the city and then take Charles to Reims so that he could receive his crown.

Because she trusted the saints, Joan did as she was asked. She walked to a nearby town and told a captain of the fort there that she would save France. She wanted him to give her an army. At first he laughed at her, but she kept asking him. While she waited for his reply, Duke Charles of Lorraine gave her a horse. Finally, the captain of the fort gave her soldiers. For safety traveling through enemy territory, she cut off her hair and wore men's clothing.

When Charles heard that a maiden from Domrémy had come to help him, he fell to the floor laughing. Still, he said that he would see her. But first he exchanged clothes with one of the men in the room. If this maiden truly has magical powers, he said, she would know him no matter what he was wearing.

Joan was led into the room. Without hesitating, she went straight to Charles and bowed. "God give you life, gentle king," she said.

"I am not the king, Joan," Charles replied. He pointed to the man wearing his clothes. "There is the king."

"By God, gentle prince, it is you and none other," Joan said.

With these words, Charles knew that there was something special about Joan. He listened as she told him her plan to save France. Charles was desperate, so he put her in command of his small army. He gave her a suit of armor and told her to do what she could.

Joan of Arc is captured by the troops of the Duke of Burgundy.

In April of 1429, Joan led the army to a bridge outside of Orléans. The English were on the other side of the bridge. There were many more English soldiers than French, but Joan was not afraid. The Lord was on her side, she told her men. God would protect them.

For hours, the French army fought the English. Finally, the French were ready to give up. Joan begged for a little more time. She jumped on her horse and raced toward the bridge. When the English saw Joan coming toward them, they were terrified. They began crowding back onto the bridge. Many fell into the water and died. The rest of the army fled. The British had been defeated, and Orléans was free once more!

Not long after this victory, Joan and Charles began their journey to Reims. Soon Charles was crowned king and the people of France celebrated.

The saints came to Joan in Reims and told her it was time to return home. But Joan had promised to continue helping the French. She said that she couldn't leave until all was well with France. The saints warned Joan that she would be taken prisoner if she stayed, but Joan felt she had no choice.

The next day, Joan was captured by the Duke of Burgundy, just as her saints had warned. The English brought her to the prison here at Rouen. She was here five months. People gathered outside and screamed that she was a witch.

The English accused Joan of heresy because she claimed to be carrying out the commands of God. In so doing, she had ignored the commands of the Church. The Church already had terrible problems and did not need the added trouble of a peasant girl who was able to hear voices from God.

At her trial, Joan said to the judge: "You say you are my judge. Consider well what you are about, for in truth I am sent from God, and you are putting yourself in great danger." The judge ignored Joan's warning and sentenced her to burn.

That night, the saints came to Joan for the last time. She cried when she saw them and said that she was afraid to die. Saint Michael replied, "Have no fear, Joan. Soon you will join us in the Kingdom of Heaven." With these words, Joan felt at peace.

This was the story that Joan of Arc told me. I believe that she spoke only the truth. At the last moment, before they took her away, I gave Joan a little cross that I had made from two small sticks. Joan smiled at me, kissed the cross, and hid it in her robe. Then the guards led her up some steps to the stake. She was still only a girl, but her work was done. She had saved France.

QUESTIONS TO CONSIDER
1. Why did Joan decide to save France?
2. Why do you think the English hated Joan?
3. What qualities did Joan have that made her a hero?

Charges Against Joan of Arc

The original list of charges against Joan included seventy things and took two days to read. These charges were later reduced to twelve. Among them were:

(1) Joan claimed she heard and saw saints and angels.

(2) Joan claimed to know future events.

(3) Joan wore men's clothing.

(4) Joan had risked her life by jumping from a high tower trying to escape.

(5) Joan said she would not obey the Church if she were ordered to do something against what her heavenly voices told her.

Beyond the Myth:
The Story of Joan of Arc
by Polly Schoyer Brooks

Polly Schoyer Brooks's biography explores the human being behind the legends of Joan of Arc.

Armor
by Charlotte and David Yue

Joan of Arc's armor had to be custom made to fit her woman's figure—it wasn't one size fits all. The Yues present a complete account of knights and armor in medieval Europe and look at the use of armor in other cultures.

The Hundred Years' War
William W. Lace

The story of Joan of Arc was an episode in the struggle between England and France known as the Hundred Years' War. William Lace describes the conflict and explains how its results were felt everywhere in Europe.

What Life Was Like

We All Fall Down

BY DEE MASTERS

The plague had come to the village where Jean (zhahn) lived. Papa had gotten sick after returning from the ship and had died in two days. Mother said she was going to get the doctor. She never came back. Jean had gone to search for her. Everyone was leaving the village. Jean followed. He passed the large pit where bodies had been thrown, one on top of the other. At the next village, men with pitchforks would not let him enter. They were burning bodies outside of that village. The ashes blew into Jean's face, and he ran.

Now there was a dead woman lying in the middle of the street. Jean walked as far from the body as he could. The body had torn clothes. Many people burning with the fever would tear off their clothing. The egg-sized swellings, the

An image of the Dance of Death from the Middle Ages.

buboes, under the arms, at the neck, and where the legs met the body, had burst. The body had large red and black blotches on it.

"Who's out there?" roared a man stepping into the deserted street from a nearby tavern. The man carried a large bunch of flowers in one hand and a **tankard** in the other. The pockets of his coat were stuffed with flowers, rosemary, and other sweet-smelling herbs. When he wasn't drinking, he stuck his face in the flowers.

"I'm hungry, sir," Jean almost whispered.

"Well, boy," the man laughed, "we shall all eat in paradise soon!" The man stumbled closer to Jean who took a step backwards. A hand grabbed weakly at his ankle. He whipped around.

The woman who had been lying in the road was not dead. She was weakly half sitting up. She fell forward, grabbing Jean's leg. He couldn't move.

"Please," she said, "water, for the love of Jesus!"

The man from the tavern pushed Jean away from the dying woman. "No water, my girl," he

---

People and Terms to Know

buboes (BOO•bohs)—swellings of the lymph glands.
tankard (TANG•kuhrd)—large cup with a single handle.

said as he knelt beside her and poured ale from his tankard across her mouth, most of it spilling down her neck. The man continued, "We are all coming with you." He looked up at Jean. "It's the end, you know. The end of the world!" The man lifted the dying woman to her feet. "Let me dance with death!" he shouted. He danced around the street, carrying the dying woman with him. "Paugh!" the man spit out as he let the woman slide back to the ground. "You stink worse than the foulest scum!" The man pulled some of the sweet-smelling herbs from his pocket and covered his face with them. He turned and staggered away.

"Let me dance with death!"

The dying woman called, "Jean? Jean!"

Jean knelt by the woman, "Who are you?" he whispered.

"Jean," she gasped. Jean had found his mother. He stood quickly and stuck the back of his hand over his mouth to keep in the scream. He turned and ran down the empty street. He almost tripped on a dead dog. He ran past empty houses with open doors. He stopped to catch his breath, leaning against a house with heavy wooden bars nailed across the windows and doors. A large red cross had been painted on its front.

A faint voice from inside the house cried, "Help me."

"Who are you?" Jean asked, leaning his cheek against the boards nailed across the door.

"I'm Susana," a young girl's voice replied. "Help me get out!"

"This is a plague house. The **parish** officers have boarded it up." Jean answered.

"No!" She cried. "No! I don't have the plague. They boarded me in with my mother and sister. Everyone is dead, except me. There is no food or water. Help me."

Jean pulled on the boards across the door and then those at the window. The heavy nails held them firmly in place.

"Help!" he called.

A man walked calmly down the street. Jean raced toward him. The man held up his hand to signal Jean to stay away. "You must leave," the man said.

"No," Jean shouted, "there's a girl . . . ."

People and Terms to Know

parish (PAR•ihsh)—district that has its own church in some Christian faiths. The word is also used to mean the members of that church.

"We're all dead," the man interrupted Jean. "I have done everything. I ate powdered emeralds. I didn't sleep during the day. How can we fight against the stars? They have caused the earth itself to breathe out poison."

"But we're all right," Jean said.

"Look here, boy!" the man said, pointing to a rosy rash in a ring around his neck. I'll be dead in three days. Now, leave!" Jean turned and ran, past a dead body floating in the mill pond, through a field dotted with golden daffodils and a hundred dead sheep rotting in the warm spring sun. He ran on into the night and the next morning. He was burning with the heat of running when he entered the next town.

In the town square, fifty men stood in a circle. They sang hymns as they beat themselves on the back with whips studded with nails. Blood gushed from their many wounds as the spikes tore their flesh. Some women had cloths ready to catch the blood and smear it on themselves. One woman cried that it was blood that would save them all. The leader of the men shouted to the townspeople that the Jews had caused the plague and must be punished. Several men dragged a dark-haired man out of a shop. Women and men beat on him until he no longer moved. Jean ran. At the edge of town he stumbled and fell to the ground. A group of small children were playing nearby.

"Ring around the rosy, a pocket full of posies, ashes, ashes, we all fall down," they sang as they danced and laughed, holding hands in their circle. One little girl broke away and ran over to Jean. Lying on the grass, he saw her sweet face looking down at him, the sun shining through her golden hair. Then she smiled and spoke in a baby's voice.

"Do you want to play with us?"

"I can't play your games," he said.

"But you can," she replied sweetly. "You can fall down. And you have a rosy ring around your neck."

Jean's hand went to his throat. He could feel the rash. He stood up and joined the children. They danced in their circle, singing, "Ring around the rosy, pocket full of posies, ashes, ashes." They all fell down.

QUESTIONS TO CONSIDER

1. What were people in the story doing to avoid getting the plague?

2. What do you think Jean should have done when he found his mother?

3. How would you have felt if you had lived through the plague?

A Medieval Celebration

BY JUDITH LLOYD YERO

My name is Niccolo, although no one in the future will remember me. It is enough that, hundreds of years from now, they will marvel at my work. Perhaps I exaggerate. The work is truly that of my master, **Orcagna**. *Artist* is a weak word for my master's many talents. He is a painter, sculptor, poet, and architect. He also creates mosaics, pictures from small pieces of colored glass.

People and Terms to Know

Orcagna (awr•KAHN•yuh)—(c. 1308–1368) Florentine artist. His real name was Andrea di Cione. With his three brothers, he was responsible for paintings, sculptures, and mosaics in churches around Florence, Italy. His most famous sculpture is the tabernacle at the church of Orsanmichele. (See the picture on the next page.) He also directed the building of the Florence Cathedral.

Andrea Orcagna's tabernacle.

It would be horrible to say that the great plague that took so many of my friends over ten years ago was a good thing. I must admit, however, that the death of so many artists and craftsmen gave me the chance to do the work I now enjoy. As a member of the stonecutter's **guild**, it is my great fortune to have been chosen to work in Orcagna's workshop, the most important art workshop in Florence, Italy. There, under his direction, we create works of art for the greatest churches in Florence.

Since the plague, there has been little to celebrate. Today, however, we will sing, dance, and feast. For the first time, people will see the finished **tabernacle** at the Church of Orsanmichele (awr•SAHN•mee•KAY•lee).

The children are very excited, as is my wife, Rosalia. Our little house is crowded because my cousin and his family have arrived from the country for the celebration. My cousin, Taddeo (TAD•day•oh),

---

People and Terms to Know

guild (gihld)—in the Middle Ages, an association of workers in a particular trade or craft. Guilds set standards for the quality of their work, described the training by which an apprentice could become a full member, and protected businesses from outside competition.

tabernacle (TAB•uhr•NAK•uhl)—place of worship. Sometimes it is a recess in a wall for a statue or relic; at other times it is a highly decorated structure that stands alone.

admires the sturdy walls of my house and the windows that bring light to the room. Although my cousin's life has improved since the plague, Taddeo and his family still live in a **wattle and daub** cottage with a dirt floor and no light but that of the fire.

"Why do you need a window?" I joke. "To let in the dark of night?" Taddeo and his family work from dawn to dusk in the fields tending their master's cattle. By the time they return for their evening meal, the sun has already gone to bed!

My wife and daughters bustle about, checking the loaves of coarse bread baking on the stone hearth. Fragrant smells rise from the **frumenty** bubbling in the pot hanging above the fire. As the women bring the food to the table, Taddeo gives us a wonderful gift of spoons that he carved from the horns of the cattle they tend on their land.

This day of celebration is a rare day off for my wife and me. For the last four years, I have left my house early each morning. I have spent my days

---

People and Terms to Know

wattle and daub (WAHT•uhl; dawb)—sticks interwoven with twigs or branches (wattle) as a framework for plaster, clay, or mud (daub).

frumenty (FROO•muhn•tee)—pudding of hulled wheat boiled in milk and flavored with sugar, spices, and raisins.

shaping and carving marble for the tabernacle with my tools. After my wife finishes her baking and adds vegetables and herbs to our evening stew, she joins me at the workshop. Her days are spent cutting tiny pieces of glass for the great rose window that our master is making for the church. This work is better done by the smaller fingers of women.

Her days are spent cutting tiny pieces of glass for the great rose window.

After filling our bellies, I dress in my finest trousers and jacket. Taddeo's clothing is made from the coarser wool his wife weaves, and we laugh at his hat with its stylish feather. Rosalia and Taddeo's wife, Maria, tuck their hair beneath their **wimples** and smooth their skirts. My daughters, their hair flying free, fasten pretty pins to their colorful wool robes.

At last, we are ready. The streets are already crowded and noisy. Musicians with flutes and stringed instruments play for coins. Street vendors have set up their colorful displays of wares— brightly dyed wools, pottery, leatherwork, and flowers. The greengrocer's bins overflow with

People and Terms to Know

wimples (WIHM•puhls)—cloths wound around the head and drawn into folds under the chin. They were worn by married women in the Middle Ages.

onions, cabbage, leeks, and herbs. Their tempting odors mix with the not so pleasant smells of garbage rotting in alleyways.

As we pass his shop, Bruno the **apothecary** calls out a welcome, his fat belly covered with the finest linens. Bruno is another who benefited from the plague that ended so many lives. He became rich selling the healing herbs that people believed would ward off the sickness.

My master used the many offerings of jewels, gold, and other riches given to the church during the plague.

Soon we join the crowds at Orsanmichele. Many stay outside to admire the statues of the saints all around the outside of the church. We hurry inside, knowing that this is where the real art lies. In his design for this memorial, my master used the many offerings of jewels, gold, and other riches given to the church during the plague. The people who made the offerings hoped that their gifts would somehow spare them from sickness and death. If they were spared, they will like the way their gifts have been used. If not, they are not likely to care one way or the other!

People and Terms to Know

apothecary (uh•PAHTH•ih•KEHR•ee)—person who prepares and sells medicines.

People stop in awe when they first see the great altar. Gold, deep blue gemstones, and the finest marble shimmer in the candlelight. In the center of the altar is a glorious painting of the **Madonna and Child**. Once again, I marvel at the brilliance of my master, Orcagna. So cleverly did he cause the pieces of marble to be joined with copper and lead that the entire tabernacle looks to be carved from a single piece of marble.

As magnificent as it is, the front of the great altar is only the beginning. As we walk around the altar, I once again feel pride in the many carved scenes from the life of the Virgin Mary. I point out the ones on which I worked to my cousins and family.

On the back of the altar, another surprise awaits, a glorious sculpture showing the death of Mary. She is also shown being taken up into heaven. Here, Orcagna has added a nice touch, for it is his own face on one of the **Apostles** shown at the Lady's death. We all note how the master's carving has changed

---

People and Terms to Know

Madonna and Child—Mary, the mother of Jesus, and the infant Jesus.
Apostles (uh•PAHS•uhls)—twelve men chosen by Jesus to preach Christianity to the world.

since the great plague. It is better and shows the pain that people know can come in an instant to destroy lives and families.

As the crowds increase and words of praise fill the church, we leave to join the festivities in the town. My wife and daughters, along with Taddeo's family, will remember the joyous events of this day for many years. As for me, my joy and pride lie in being one of many who worked on this great building. We have created something that will outlive us by hundreds of years.

My life is good. I have survived the Black Death and lived to see my family strong and healthy. Even after our death, Orcagna and those of us who worked on his masterpieces will live on for years and years in the churches and shrines of Florence.

QUESTIONS TO CONSIDER

1. Why was the plague a good thing for Niccolo?

2. What are some differences between the way city people and country people lived?

3. Where did the materials used to decorate the tabernacle come from?

4. What do you think were the best and worst things about living during the Middle Ages?

That Business Called Marriage

BY BARBARA LITTMAN

The cafeteria was so crowded that Mary could barely make her way to the table. She was carrying soup for Charlie and a veggie burger for herself. Charlie had his head buried in the student newspaper, reading the article he'd written about high school students who were being raised just by their moms.

"Hey, how 'bout some help here?" she teased him when she got closer. He looked up a little startled and then gave her his oh-so-Charlie sheepish grin. He folded up the paper quickly and took the tray out of her hands.

Mary liked Charlie better than just about any guy she'd ever met. He was funny, in a sly sort of way, and smart, and lots of fun to argue with.

An image of lovers in a garden from the Middle Ages.

She sat down and took the food off the tray. "Well, what do you think? Is it as good in print as it was when I saw the rough draft?"

"I think so," Charlie replied. "But I still wish I could have gotten a better quote from the mom who was divorced. She made it sound like her marriage had just been a business arrangement that didn't work out."

> "She made it sound like her marriage had just been a business arrangement that didn't work out."

"Well, what's so shocking about that? That's pretty much what marriage was for centuries. If the couple fell in love after they got married, they were the lucky ones," Mary said.

"Oh, come on," Charlie argued. "You're exaggerating. Arranged marriages are in places like China and India, not in Western countries."

"Oh boy," Mary thought. "This is just the kind of discussion I like." Reaching down to unzip her backpack, she gave Charlie a sly little smile.

"Are you sure?" she said. "Or do you want to take it back before I prove you wrong?" She set two books from her women's studies class on the table—*The Illustrated Letters of the Paston Family* and *The Pastons and Their England*.

"Okay, I know when I'm doomed," laughed Charlie. "What do you have there?"

"Proof of how wrong you are!" said Mary. "These are the letters of the **Paston family**. They lived in the Middle Ages, and the letters are so cool. There are letters here between lawyers and heads of households, between husbands and wives, parents and children, and friends. By reading them, you can find out how people lived in the 1400s. There's tons of stuff about marriage."

"Yeah? So what does it say?" asked Charlie.

"Well, marriages were arranged by the parents and set up like any business deal. Marriage was a way for families to increase their wealth. Often the family would own more property after a marriage, or they might get a lot of money from a **dowry**." Mary opened *The Pastons and Their England*.

> The problem of arranging a marriage for one or another of the family seems seldom to have left the minds of the elder members, yet almost always without any direct reference to the person concerned.

People and Terms to Know

Paston family—English family of the 1400s, whose letters have been preserved and serve as valuable historical documents today.

dowry (DOW•ree)—money or property brought by a bride to her husband at marriage.

"Here's part of a letter about Sir John Paston's sister, Anne. Keep in mind, she didn't know a thing about any of this while it was going on." Mary started reading the chapter on marriage.

If your sister be not married, I trust God I know where she may be married to a gentleman of 400 marks of livelode [livelihood], the which is a great gentleman born and of good blood.

"But, what's really amazing," Mary went on, "is that John Paston found out the 'great gentleman' was trying to marry off a young man so he could get the dowry for himself. When the young man said he wouldn't turn it over, the 'great gentleman' lost all interest in the negotiations."

"Okay, okay, you've made your point," Charlie admitted. "But because marriages were usually business deals, did no one ever marry for love?"

"Well, there is one exception I know about," said Mary. "It was Margery Brews and John Paston III, the younger brother of the guy I was just talking about. It's a pretty sweet story.

They met just before Valentine's Day, and it sounds like love at first sight. Listen to this. She wrote him a Valentine letter. This was in 1477.

Right reverent and worshipful and my right well beloved Valentine, I recommend me unto you, full heartily desiring to hear of your welfare.

"That's pretty forward. Most women at that time barely knew their husbands before they got married. Anyway, then she ends the letter:

And if it please you to hear of my welfare, I am not in good health of body, nor heart, nor shall be till I hear from you . . .

"I think it's fair to say she was smitten," Mary laughed.

"Did they ever get married?" Charlie asked.

"It took a lot of negotiating. Margery knew her father wouldn't pay a big dowry because she had two sisters who also needed dowries. Here, listen to this letter just a few days after the Valentine letter.

I will let you plainly know that my father will no more part with in that behalf, but **pounds** and **marks**, which is right far from the accomplishment you desire. Wherefore, if you could be content with that good

---

People and Terms to Know

pounds and **marks**—units of English money.

money and my poor person, I would be the merriest maiden on earth. . .

"Margery's mother, Dame Elizabeth, supported the marriage, so that helped," Mary went on to say. "At one point John even got Dame Elizabeth and his mother together for dinner so they could have what John called 'most secret talking.'

"Eventually, Margery's father agreed to pay two hundred marks and give the couple free room and board for three years. They got married in December. So it took eight months of working out a deal until they could get married. They married for love, but it was still a business deal."

"Pretty far out," Charlie said. "And speaking of business deals, I insist on paying for my own soup."

Mary laughed. "I don't accept. I like it that you owe me. Don't worry," she said, pushing back her chair. "I'll collect."

QUESTIONS TO CONSIDER

1. Why was the marriage between Margery Brews and John Paston unusual for its day?

2. What were the main reasons people married at the time of the Pastons?

3. How do the reasons people marry today differ from those of people like the Pastons in the Middle Ages?

Sources

An Emperor's Vision *by Dee Masters*

Caius and Titus are fictional characters. Constantine and Maxentius are historical figures. A good source for this time period is *The Decline and Fall of the Roman Empire* by Edward Gibbon (Chicago: Encyclopaedia Britannica, 1989).

Attila and the Pope *by Walter Hazen*

The narrator is fictional. All the people named in the story are real historical figures. The details in the story are historically accurate. An interesting account of the meeting between Pope Leo and Attila can be found in *The Age of Faith* by Will Durant (New York: Simon and Schuster, 1950).

A Bear-Keeper's Daughter *by Stephen Feinstein*

Juliana and the scribe Thanasis are fictional characters. Justinian, Theodora, Belisarius, and Akakios are all historical figures. Sources include *Theodora: Portrait in a Byzantine Landscape* by Anthony Bridge (Chicago, IL: Academy Chicago Publishers, 1984) and *What Life Was Like Amid Splendor and Intrigue: The Byzantine Empire 330–1453,* by the editors of Time-Life Books (Alexandria, VA: Time-Life Books, 1998).

Work—*The Rule* of St. Benedict *by Dee Masters*

The people in this story are historical figures and the events are historically accurate. Sources include *The Life of St. Benedict* by St. Gregory the Great, commentary by Adalbert de Vogue, OSB (Petersham, MA: St. Bede's Publications); *St. Benedict* by Justin McCann, OSB (Franklin, WI: Sheed & Ward); and *Benedict of Nursia* by Patrick O'Donovan (London: William Collins & Sons). Benedict's *Rule,* an important document in Western civilization, can be read in *The Rule of Saint Benedict: In English* edited by Timothy Fry (Vintage Books, 1998).

Viking Raiders *by Judith Lloyd Yero*

The narrator is a fictional character. All other people mentioned are real. The story is based on the battle of Maldon, which took place on the southeast coast of England in 991. Quotes about the battle are taken from a translation of the Anglo-Saxon poem "The Battle of Maldon" by Charles Abbott Conway. You can read the entire poem in either a modern translation or in Anglo-Saxon from various sources on the Internet. A good source of information on the other characters and the history of the Vikings is *Viking Life* by John Guy (Hauppage, NY: Barron's Educational Series, Inc., 1998).

Muhammad the Messenger *by Barbara Littmann*

All the people in this story are historical figures, and the events told come to us from ancient Islamic historical traditions, the earliest of which date from about 125 years after the death of the Prophet. The primary Arabic biography was written in the 700s by Ishaq. It can be read in a translation by Ibn Hisham, *The Life of Muhammad: A Translation of Ishaq's Sirat Rasul Allah*. Other sources include *Muhammad, His Life Based on the Earliest Sources* (Rochester, NY: Inner Traditions, 1983) and *The Oxford History of Islam*, John L. Esposito, editor (New York: Oxford University Press, 2000).

Charlemagne and the Pope *by Stephen Currie*

The *Frankish Post-Gazette* is, of course, fiction. The facts it reports in its news stories, however, are historically accurate. You can read more about Charlemagne in *Charlemagne* by Richard Winston and the editors of *Horizon Magazine* (New York: American Heritage Publishing Co., Inc., 1968).

Avicenna, Prince of Philosophy *by Walter Hazen*

Guido, the narrator, Silvio, and Maria are fictional characters. Avicenna, Galen, and the emir of Bukhara are real. A source for this story was *Early Islam* by Desmond Stewart (New York: Time-Life, 1967).

Bad King John *by Stephen Feinstein*

The narrator, his grandson Gavin, and Old William are fictional characters. King John, King Henry II, Eleanor of Aquitaine, Richard the Lion-Hearted, and Arthur are historical figures. A source for the information in this story is *The Life and Times of King John* by Maurice Ashley (London: Weidenfeld and Nicolson, 1972).

St. Thomas Aquinas Kidnapped *by Lynnette Brent*

The letter-writing friar and his sister are fictional characters. The content of the letters, however, reflects actual events in the life of St. Thomas. A source for this story is *St. Thomas Aquinas: The Story of the Dumb Ox* by Mary Fabyan Windeatt and Mary J. Dorcy (Rockford, IL: Tan Books and Publishers, 1994).

The Pardoner's Tale *by Stephen Currie*

This story is a modern retelling of the story from Geoffrey Chaucer's *Canterbury Tales*. Chaucer was a government official and poet who wrote these stories between 1386 and 1400. The details and point of view of the story give an accurate picture of life at the time. Chaucer's *Tales* is one of the classic works of English literature. A Modern Library edition of Chaucer's work was published in 1994.

The Maid of Orléans *by Marianne McComb*

The priest and his account of Joan's final hours are fictional. They are based on information from two books: *Beyond the Myth: The Story of Joan of Arc* by Polly Schoyer Brooks (Boston: Houghton Mifflin Co., 1999) and *Joan of Arc* by Mary Gordon (New York: Viking Press, 2000).

We All Fall Down *by Dee Masters*

Jean is a fictional character and his story is fiction. However, the details about the bubonic plague and people's reactions during its height are all too real. They are vividly described in many documents from the period. A source is *The Black Death: Natural and Human Disaster in Medieval Europe* (New York: Free Press, 1983).

A Medieval Celebration *by Judith Lloyd Yero*

The narrator and his family members are fictional. Orcagna was a real artist, sculptor, and architect of the time. The description of his work is accurate. Details about life in medieval times can be found in *Medieval Life* by Andrew Langley, (New York: Alfred A. Knopf, 1996).

That Business Called Marriage *by Barbara Littmann*

Mary and Charlie are fictional characters. Margery Brews and John Paston and their letters are real. Sources include *Illustrated Letters of the Paston Family: Private Life in the Fifteenth Century* edited by Roger Virgoe (London: Macmillan), *The Pastons and Their England: Studies in an Age of Transition* by H. S. Bennet (Cambridge, England: The University Press, 1922), and *A Medieval Family: The Pastons of Fifteenth-Century England* by Frances and Joseph Gies (New York: HarperCollins Publishers, 1998).

Glossary of People and Terms to Know

Apostles (uh•PAHS•uhls)—twelve men chosen by Jesus to preach Christianity to the world.

apothecary (uh•PAHTH•ih•KEHR•ee)—person who prepares and sells medicines.

Arabs (AR•uhbs)—people of the large southwest Asian country of Arabia, where Muhammad was born.

Attila (AT•uhl•uh)—(c. 406–453) king of the Huns after 434. He destroyed cities from the Danube River in central and eastern Europe to the Rhine River in Germany.

Avicenna (AV•ih•SEHN•uh)— (980–1037) Arab doctor and philosopher, born in Bukhara, a city in central Asia. His medical book, the *Canon of Medicine,* was used in Europe until the 1600s.

barbaric (bahr•BAR•ihk)—not civilized; rude and wild. According to the Romans, anyone who lived outside the Roman Empire was barbaric or a barbarian.

Belisarius (BEHL•ih•SAIR•ee•uhs)— (c. 505–565) powerful Byzantine general whose loyalty to Justinian and Theodora prevented rebels from overthrowing them in the Nika Revolt of 532.

Benedict (BEHN•ih•DIHKT)— (c. 480–547) Italian monk and founder of the Benedictine order of monks. His *Rule* became a guide-book for monks for centuries.

bread and wine—very small amount of food and drink used in the Christian Communion, a ceremony to remember Christ's last supper.

buboes (BOO•bohs)—swellings of the lymph glands.

Canterbury (KAN•tuhr•BEHR•ee) —town in southern England. In the cathedral, or large church, at Canterbury is the tomb of Saint Thomas á Becket. He had been a high official in the Church who had been murdered there. The tomb attracted many pilgrims.

Carloman (CAHRL•uh•MAHN)—(751–771) son of Pepin the Short. With his brother Charlemagne, he ruled the Franks until his death.

cavalry (KAV•uhl•ree)—soldiers who fight on horseback.

Charlemagne (SHAHR•luh•MAYN) —(c. 741–814) king of the Franks from 768 to his death. He was crowned Roman Emperor of the West in 800. His name means "Charles the Great."

Charles VII—(1403–1461) king of France. He fought England for the right to rule. With the help of Joan of Arc, he was crowned in 1429 and ruled until his death.

circus—place where large enter-tainments were put on free for the Roman public.

Constantine (KAHN•stuhn•TEEN) —(c. 285–337) Roman emperor from 306 to 337. He moved the capital east to Constantinople, ended persecution of Christians, and supported the spread of Christianity.

consul—official of the Roman government.

Crusades—military expeditions undertaken by Christian powers to win the Holy Land from the Muslims. There were Crusades in the 1000s, 1100s, and 1200s.

Danegeld (DAYN•gehld)—"tax of the Danes," gold, silver, and other goods paid to the Vikings in exchange for not being attacked. The English people were heavily taxed to pay for Danegeld.

dowry (DOW•ree)—money or property brought by a bride to her husband at marriage.

Eleanor of Aquitaine (AK•wih•TAYN)—(c. 1122–1204) queen of France (1137–1152) and queen of England (1152–1204).

emir (ih•MIHR)—prince or chieftain in the Middle East.

Erik Bloodaxe (died 954)—Viking who was named king of parts of England by the Norwegians.

Ethelred (EHTH•uhl•REHD)—(c. 968–1016) Ethelred II, called "Ethelred the Unready," king of England from 978 to 1016. His struggles against the Danes were unsuccessful.

Franks—Germanic people whose territory, in Charlemagne's time, included some of present-day Germany, France, Belgium, and the Netherlands.

Frederick II—(1194–1250) Holy Roman emperor from 1220 to 1250; great patron of artists and thinkers.

frumenty (FROO•muhn•tee)—pudding of hulled wheat boiled in milk and flavored with sugar, spices, and raisins.

Galen (GAY•luhn)—(c. 130–c. 200) Greek doctor and writer.

Gaul (gawl)—ancient region of western Europe that was part of the Roman Empire. It included all of what is now France and surrounding areas.

guild (gihld)—in the Middle Ages, an association of workers in a particular trade or craft. Guilds set standards for the quality of their work, described the training by which an apprentice could become a full member, and protected businesses from outside competition.

heathen (HEE•thuhn)—people thought to be uncivilized; often used to mean those who are not Christians.

Henry II—(1133–1189) king of England (1154–1189). A strong king who expanded England's territory in Wales and Ireland, he is best known for expressing his shame publicly after some of his knights murdered Archbishop Thomas à Becket, with whom he had quarreled.

heretic (HEHR•ih•tihk)—person who disagrees with the established beliefs of a church. The opinion of that person is called heresy (HEHR•ih•see).

Hijra (hih•JEE•ruh)—flight of Muhammad from Mecca to Medina in 622. Its date marks the beginning of the Islamic calendar.

Hippodrome—stadium in Constantinople seating 60,000 spectators and offering free entertainment, such as chariot races and trained animal acts.

Huns—nomadic, warring people from north-central Asia who occupied China. About 370, they moved west.

illuminated (ih•LOO•muh•NAYT•uhd) **manuscripts**—hand copied books with very bright lettering and decorations, usually made by monks before the invention of the printing press.

Ivar (EYE•vahr) **the Boneless**— (794–872) Danish Viking leader who ruled Dublin and later captured York in England.

Joan of Arc—(c. 1412–1431) French peasant girl who led a successful defeat of the English at Orléans in 1429.

John—(1167–1216) king of England from 1199 to 1216. He was the son of Henry II and Eleanor of Aquitaine.

Justinian (juh•STIHN•ee•un)— (483–565) brilliant emperor of the Eastern Empire from 527 to 565. He was a great builder, and the preserver of Roman law for future generations.

Ka'bah (KAH•buh)—most sacred shrine in the Islamic world. It is toward the Ka'bah that Muslims turn when they pray.

legions (LEE•juhns)—companies of 3,000 to 6,000 foot soldiers and 300 to 700 men on horseback.

Leo I—(c. 400–461) pope known as "Leo the Great." He was pope from 440 to 461. He saved Rome from an invasion of the Huns in 452. He persuaded the leader of the Vandals, a German tribe, to spare the city again three years later.

Leo III—pope from 795 to 816. His enemies accused him of selling Church jobs to the highest bidder and of other immoral behaviors. He was attacked by his enemies in 799.

Madonna and Child—Mary, the mother of Jesus, and the infant Jesus.

Magna Carta (MAG•nuh KAHR•tuh)—Latin for "Great Charter." English document that is the basis for our modern system of justice. Among other things, it granted the right to a trial by jury and established that the law is more important than the king.

Maxentius (mak•SEHN•shee•uhs) —co-ruler with Constantine of the Western Roman Empire. He controlled Italy and Rome itself.

Mecca (MEH•kuh)—city in Arabia where Muhammad grew up. Mecca is a holy city for Muslim believers.

miracles (MIHR•uh•kuhls)— unusual events that cannot be explained by science.

monastery (MAHN•uh•STEHR•ee) —community or building where monks live.

monk—man who gives up worldly things and enters a monastery to live a religious life.

Monte Cassino (MAHN•tee kuh•SEE•noh)—mountain in Italy and site of a famous monastery.

Muhammad (mu•HAM•ihd)— (c. 570–632) prophet and founder of Islam, the religion of the Muslims.

Muslims—people who accept Muhammad's teachings and follow the five pillars of a good Muslim life.

Orcagna (awr•KAHN•yuh)— (c. 1308–1368) Florentine artist. His real name was Andrea di Cione. With his three brothers, he was responsible for paintings, sculptures, and mosaics in churches around Florence, Italy. His most famous sculpture is the tabernacle at the church of Orsanmichele. He also directed the building of the Florence Cathedral.

order—group of religious persons, such as monks, living together.

Orléans (awr•lay•AHN)—city of north-central France.

parchment—skin of a sheep or goat prepared as a material on which to write.

pardoner (PAHR•duhn•uhr)—in the Middle Ages, a church official. In Geoffrey Chaucer's *Canterbury Tales*, a pardoner is one of a group of people on the way to Canterbury.

parish (PAR•ihsh)—district that has its own church in some Christian faiths. The word is also used to mean the members of that church.

Paston family—English family of the 1400s whose letters have been preserved and serve as valuable historical documents today.

Pepin (PEHP•ihn) **the Short**— (c. 714–768) Charlemagne's father and king of the Franks from 751–768.

persecution (PUHR•sih•KYOO•shuhn)—bad treatment of people because of their principles or beliefs.

petitions (puh•TISH•uns)—formal requests for rights or benefits from an authority. A petitioner is someone who makes such a request.

pilgrimage (PIL•gruh•mihj)— journey to a sacred place or shrine.

pilgrims—people who go on a journey to a religious place for religious reasons.

plague (playg)—disease that spreads quickly and usually causes death. One of the worst kinds of plague is the bubonic plague, which is caused by fleas carried by rats.

pounds and marks—units of English money.

prophet (PRAH•fuht)—religious leader through whom the will of God is spoken.

Qur'an (kuh•RAN)—sacred text considered by Muslims to contain the revelations of God to Muhammad. It is sometimes spelled *Koran*.

relic (REHL•ihk)—part of the body or object belonging to a holy person and kept as something to be honored.

revelations (REHV•uh•LAY•shuns) —truths that God revealed to the prophets. Muhammad's reports of his revelations form the basis for Islam.

Richard the Lion-Hearted (1157–1199)—king of England from 1189 to 1199. He is more well known for his bravery as a soldier than as a ruler.

runes (roons)—letters in an ancient alphabet used by the Scandinavians.

Runnymede (RUHN•nee•meed) —meadow west of London on the south bank of the Thames River where the Magna Carta was signed in 1215.

sagas (SAH•guhs)—long stories about brave Viking kings and fighters, their families, and their gods.

Saxons—Germanic people who were neighbors to the north and east of the Franks. Unlike the Franks, they were not Christians.

Scandinavia—Norway, Sweden, and Denmark.

scribe—in ancient times, a public clerk. People who did not know how to read or write would use a scribe to help them.

serfs—workers who could not legally leave the estate of the lord they worked for.

tabernacle (TAB•uhr•NAK•uhl)—
place of worship. Sometimes it is a
recess in a wall for a statue
or relic; at other times it is a
highly decorated structure that
stands alone.

tankard (TANG•kuhrd)—large
cup with a single handle.

Theodora (thee•uh•DAW•ruh)—
(c. 508–548) wife of the emperor
Justinian. She had great influence
over him and over the political and
religious events of their rule.

theology (thee•AWL•uh•jee)—
study of religious faith and
experience, especially the study
of God and God's relationship to
the world.

Thomas Aquinas
(uh•KWY•nuhs)—(1225–1274)
Italian student at the time of this
story. Later he became the greatest
philosopher and scholar of the
medieval Church. He wrote *Summa
Theologica*. In 1323, the Church
declared him a saint.

Thor (thawr)—Viking god who
rides through the heavens in a
chariot drawn by goats, striking
rocks with his hammer to create
lightning and thunder. Thor's
hammer was a symbol of power.

Tryggvasson, Olaf (OH•luhf
TRIG•vuh•suhn)—(968–1000)
Viking leader who, after many
raids on England, was converted to
Christianity. After becoming king
of Norway in 995, he forced his
people to accept Christianity.

Valhalla (val•HAL•uh)—in
Scandinavian mythology, the place
where heroes go after death to
spend their time eating, drinking,
and fighting.

Vatican (VAT•ih•kuhn)—government of the pope in Rome; also
the buildings that house the pope.

Vikings (VY•kihngs)—daring
sailors from Scandinavia (Norway,
Sweden, and Denmark) who raided
the coasts of Europe from around
800 until 1000. They were also
called Norsemen or Northmen.

wattle and daub (WAWT•uhl;
dawb)—method of building con-
struction using sticks interwoven
with twigs or branches (wattle)
as a framework for plaster, clay,
or mud (daub).

Western Roman Emperor—
ruler of the western part of the
old Roman Empire. The Roman
Empire had been split into eastern
and western halves around 286.

Wife of Bath—character in
Chaucer's *Canterbury Tales,* she was a
married woman from the town of
Bath in southwest England.

wimples (WIHM•puhls)—cloths
wound around the head and drawn
into folds under the chin. They were
worn by married women in the
Middle Ages.

Acknowledgements

9 © The Granger Collection.
11 © North Wind Picture Archives.
14 © Explorer, Paris/SuperStock
International.
16 © Giraudon/Art Resource, NY.
17 © Corbis.
18 © Hulton Getty Picture
Collection.
19 © The Granger Collection.
20 © Stock Montage.
23 © North Wind Picture Archives.
27 © SuperStock International.
30 © Capitoline Museums, Rome,
Italy/Canali PhotoBank, Milan/
SuperStock.
35 © Corbis/NY.
43 © Hulton Getty Picture
Collection.
49 © North Wind Picture Archives.
51 © The Granger Collection.

55 © Newberry Library/SuperStock
International.
61 © Corbis.
64 © The Granger Collection.
68 © Corbis.
71 © Saxonian State Library/
SuperStock International.
81, 86, 92 © SuperStock
International.
100 © Corbis.
105, 110 © Hulton Getty Picture
Collection.
112 © The Granger Collection.
119 © SuperStock International.
130 © The Granger Collection.
132 © Giraudon/Art Resource, NY.
134, 138, 142 © Stock Montage.
150 © Alinari/Art Resource.
158 © British Library, London/
SuperStock.